Men in Marriage

Your Wife Wants to Have a Relationship With You

TIMOTHY GALVIN, MSW

outskirts
press

Men In Marriage
Your Wife Wants To Have A Relationship With You
All Rights Reserved.
Copyright © 2024 Timothy Galvin, MSW
v2.0

The opinions expressed in this manuscript are solely the opinions of the author and do not represent the opinions or thoughts of the publisher. The author has represented and warranted full ownership and/or legal right to publish all the materials in this book.

This book may not be reproduced, transmitted, or stored in whole or in part by any means, including graphic, electronic, or mechanical without the express written consent of the publisher except in the case of brief quotations embodied in critical articles and reviews.

Outskirts Press, Inc.
http://www.outskirtspress.com

ISBN: 978-1-9772-7056-6

Library of Congress Control Number: 2023924726

Cover Photo © 2024 www.gettyimages.com. All rights reserved - used with permission.

Outskirts Press and the "OP" logo are trademarks belonging to Outskirts Press, Inc.

PRINTED IN THE UNITED STATES OF AMERICA

Introduction

Thank you for reading this book. So many things in life are about perspective and attitude. The goal of this book is to provide you with a perspective that is not typically the way men look at and approach relationships in their lives. I'm hoping that with a new (and hopefully, more helpful) perspective, you will be clearer in the way you approach and engage your wife, which will give you more confidence, connection, and hope surrounding your participation in your marriage.

I've been working with couples for forty-four years in various settings. I've been providing educational groups for men around topics and issues of marriage for the last ten years. Over Covid, when I found myself working from home and having more time on my hands, I did more reading about men in marriage and men who better understand the women in their lives. My intention in all of this is to help you understand your wife, yourself, and your marriage better.

The way I have approached writing this book is to begin each chapter with a typical question I have been asked by men over the years (some chapters have more than one question when topics seem related). These questions are the common concerns that many men have expressed to me about their wives and marriages. I'm hoping these questions are the kinds of concerns you might have about your relationship with your wife and your marriage. I have tried to be as specific as possible with my answers and ideas. I also cover a number of topics in the book. That's my writing style. I'm not sure what information resonates with any one man, so I cover a lot, hoping everyone gets something useful for them to apply to their marriage relationship. I know men (being one) can be pragmatic and concrete in their approach to many things. Hopefully, I will be able to do that with you. I also know men don't necessarily like a lot of words, so I have attempted to be succinct in my answers to each question, without losing the important content or point.

Throughout the book I refer to men in a "universal" way. There is great variation in men's temperaments and personalities. I, too, know that men may exhibit the "helpful and not-so-helpful" attitudes and behaviors I reference by varying degrees. Sometimes, it is the woman in the marriage who exhibits the attitudes and behaviors I speak about——a "reversal." In all of my examples, names have been changed to protect client confidentiality. So now, let's get started.

Table of Contents

Introduction iii

Chapter One 1

"We've been married to each other for years, so why does it feel like we're not on the same page?"

"Why is marriage so much work?"

Chapter Two 11

Say you come into my office for counseling and you say: "My wife says I don't love her, but I do! I'm worried my marriage is going to fall apart for no good reason, and I can't prevent it!"

Chapter Three 23

"Why Does it seem our serious conversations derail most anytime we talk?

Chapter Four 33

Boy code? What in the world is the 'boy code' and why is it important for me to know whether it impacts me and how?"

Why is my wife always trying to control me? Make me do what she wants?

"If my grandfathers and father were angry men in their marriages, will I be an angry man in my marriage, too?"

Chapter Five 42

"Am I afraid of my wife? If so, how can I tame my fear?"

Chapter Six 53

"My wife complains that I am always defending myself when she brings up a problem in our marriage. I don't know what she expects me to do when she blames me for things I didn't do. What's wrong with me defending myself when she is wrong about me?"

"Ok, that was defensiveness, what about avoidance? What's that about?"

Chapter Seven 62

"I said I was sorry, why doesn't she believe me?"

Chapter Eight 76

"How do I rebuild trust after a terrible mistake"? Or years of "getting it wrong"?

Chapter Nine 87

"How do I get my wife to say "YES" to sex more often?

Chapter Ten 101

"Why is she always coming at me with a list of problems?"

Chapter Eleven 112

"You automatically make a difference in your marriage.

You decide whether that difference will be the positive difference you want it to be."

Appendix A:	119
Appendix B:	122
Suggested Readings	125
References	127
Acknowledgements	131

For Kathy

The love of my life.

Chapter One

"We've been married to each other for years, so why does it feel like we're not on the same page?"

I THINK A lot of men come around to that question at some time in their marriage. The most important thing your wife wants from you is what? "She wants to have a relationship with you." I know that may seem like common knowledge, but in a marriage, what men often think a relationship is, and what women think are two different things. In men's minds a relationship is more about a series of transactional events between two people to accomplish a goal. "I do this for you…..You do this for me," and in the end it all works. I'm not saying that women don't see and practice "transactional" events in their relationships, they certainly do. Women can very much be about working together to get things done. But women see the real relationship as much more than that. They see it as an emotional, verbal, cognitive, and spiritual engagement. For women, it is not some kind of arrangement (or bargain). No, to them, it is a bond—a love relationship. When I say, "Your wife wants to have a relationship with you," I mean she wants to talk, express mutual interest in each other, be open-hearted, vulnerable and trusting, encouraging, and loving. Pretty terrifying, eh? I know, right now you're thinking: "that's all well and good, but it is just a romantic fantasy." Guys, I'm here to tell you all of these things she's looking for are possible. My goal is to show you how to be an active, vital contributor to building this kind of relationship with your wife. And, it is not just for her. We, as men, need to experience all of these things in our lives, too. And we can find them in our marriage. I know, you're thinking: "Look, I know how to make things worse between us, but I have no idea how to make things better." As you keep reading, I will cover not only the things we as men need to be aware of and stop doing (usually we have no idea what we're doing wrong), but I will also show you what you can do to connect with your wife and join her in a supportive, responsive, loving marriage.

First of all, we need to know what's important to our wives. John Gottman, who's decades of research has contributed greatly to understanding marriages, discovered that the single most important quality a woman looks for in a man (potential husband) is trustworthiness *(1)*. I was shocked at first hearing this, but when I thought about it, it made perfect sense. If a woman is looking to have a relationship with a man for her lifetime, finding someone who will look after her safety and well-being (not to mention her heart), as well as that of her future children is vitally important. She depends on the stability and trustworthiness of her husband. When you think about it, the world is often not a safe place for women. Women tend to travel in groups. They watch out for each other in the world (i.e., their drinks at parties and bars, and when they walk to their cars in parking garages and lots, just to name a few ways…) One of the FBI's largest crime categories is assaults against women between the ages of eighteen and thirty-five years old. I say this to make men aware of the fact that the world women sometimes experience is not the same world men experience.

I worked once with a very adventurous couple. They went out into the world frequently to explore places and people where the risk in their activities was higher than most other couples I knew. They came to see me because in their more recent adventures he'd walk ahead of her and not be aware of some of the physical and environmental difficulties and dangers she was experiencing at the time. She said he "did not see or appreciate the jeopardy or danger she felt at times and would just go off at his own speed not thinking about her or checking on her." When she told him what she was experiencing, he would often minimize or dismiss her concerns. He would call her names like "baby," "softie," or "drama queen." He continued to do so in our sessions, which made her point, as he "abandoned" her emotionally and psychologically repeatedly in their conversations. The trust she felt earlier in the marriage had eroded, and she left him. Trustworthiness!

In his work, Gottman never defined what constituted trustworthiness. I went to Daniel Webster to find his definition of trustworthiness. Here is what Mr. Webster had to say: "trustworthiness=worthy of trust."

Not very helpful. So, I thought about my own experience in working with couples and came up with a five-component definition of trustworthiness:

1. The husband is reliable and dependable. He can be counted on. He is responsive to the needs of his wife when she calls him.

2. The husband is predictable. He is consistent in his relationship. No negative surprises in the way he carries out his responsibilities.

3. The husband is accountable. He is open and transparent in all he does. He doesn't hide things or keep secrets from his wife. (More on this in future chapters).

4. The husband is truthful. His wife can count on what he tells her. He is worthy of her confidence.

5. The husband is safe and protective. He keeps his wife's confidences. He protects her in social situations. He is gentle, not aggressive, in his relationship with her.

I worked with a couple, Sharon and Cooper, in which the woman was "the odd one out" in her extended family. Her mother and two sisters would often "pick on her and mis-characterize her" at family events. Though this had always been part of her life with her family, Cooper didn't like it. He started the practice of talking about her positive qualities and the many competencies Sharon had in her relationship with him, and out in the world. The couple reported that as Cooper did this, some of the "stories" told by the mother and sisters didn't quite go away, but they certainly subsided, and they knew when they did bring something negative up about Sharon, Cooper would be right there to counter it with his support of her. In one of our sessions, Sharon turned to Cooper and said to him: "You're the first man in my life who ever acted to defend me and protect me, and I love you so much more for doing that for me."

As husbands we need to be aware of what we do in our marriages. Too often we just "bump along," not thinking of the messages we are sending to our wives, and the impact we are having on her. During a session, a husband declared out loud in a session with his wife: "I don't know what she's complaining about, I didn't do anything!"

I looked at him and said: "I think that's what she's complaining about." We need to pay attention and practice these five ways of being in the relationship with our wives. We love our wife. We want her to know our love and caring so she feels the reassurance we want her to have from us. It is very important for our wives to be "seen, heard, and appreciated" in our relationship. For who she is, but also for all she does for us daily (and it's usually a lot!).

Reader: "So that's it, 'do this and don't do that,' and I'm good to go?"

Galvin: "Oh, no! There is so much more and it's all good!" Because your wife wants to have a relationship with you.

"Why is marriage so much work?"

That is an interesting question. The word "work" implies "this is something I **have** to do, but don't necessarily want to." It's funny, sometimes women have asked me the very same question. But I think for women the work seems to be a different kind of work, as I will show in the "For Wives Only" section below. Let me start by saying some things about marriage.

As human beings, it is in all sorts of relationships that we find our identity and grow as people. Family relationships are the most important relationships we experience in our lifetimes. Marriage is at the center of family relationships. Marriage links two families together and connects generations. Marriage is also the most complicated of all human relationships. At one and the same time, two people are responsible to raise children, run a household, earn and manage money together, deal with the in-laws and out-laws, have a social life, and make a myriad of other kinds of decisions, all the while conducting a vibrant, romantic, love relationship. Often married couples put their love relationship on the back burner to deal with everything else they need to attend to, only to lose the one relationship they really need to give them the love and support that keeps everything else going.

So, marriage is busy. Relationships have lots of needs, hopes, and expectations, with limited time, energy, and resources. "Busy and tired" is a state many couples find themselves in. When we are "busy and tired" everything feels like work!

Actually, the reason I think men find marriage to be "so much work," is the perspective they take on the relationship. Men tend to look at relationships in a transactional way ("you do this for me, I do this for you."). Men are also content with less, and don't expect to have to do so much. Men's mantra: "Expect less, do less." Men are also more vigilant about being "put upon" (asked to do more, than expected), or be coerced to do things by others. So, with that outlook, yes, everything can look like work.

Lynn and Blake were in conflict about her doing so much more in running the household and caring for the children than was Blake. Lynn reported in every area of their lives she took care of so much more than Blake (caring for the children, running their household, managing money, and pursuing the marital relationship). She reported Blake does only as much as he thinks necessary and stops. This leaves Lynn to finish up the tasks alone. For example, Blake agreed that he would give their three young children a bath in the evenings. When he was finished, Lynn found three, mostly wet, naked children running through the house, and Blake back on his computer. The dirty clothes and wet towels were still on the bathroom floor. Dirty bath water was still in the tub; teeth weren't brushed and pajamas weren't on the kids. Lynn reported that she had gone over the fact that "giving the kids a bath is a twelve-step process from beginning to end, and Blake needed to do all twelve, if he was to be helpful." Nothing changed.

Using the word, "work" is not off by much. There is a lot to do running a household, caring for children, and earning and managing money. It's busy. It's routine. It's messy, consuming a great deal of emotional energy. It's a lot of caregiving. It's not exciting or glamorous. It requires discipline. It requires sacrifice. It's all-important. Our caring for our wives is a "work of love."

Reader: "How can we, as husbands, look at our marriages in a way that makes it seem less like "work?" We can see the "work" we do as a labor of love. We can see our marriage as being part of a team. It's a partnership. Men understand teamwork, it's just that we tend not to look at our marriage in that way. I think men tend to do better when they see themselves, and their effort, as part of something bigger than themselves. That is exactly what a marriage and family life is. We, as husbands, have to see the relationship as something in which we want to be an active contributor and for which we wish to be accountable. We play an important part. When we under-function, disengage, or act like it is not that important to us, we are letting the most important "teammate" in our lifetimes down. When we do these things, she learns not to count on us. Her feeling is "I can't believe him." He's not trustworthy. The bigger message is "He doesn't care and I'm on my own in this relationship." Never forget, your wife wants to have a relationship with you.

REMEMBER:

Your wife chose to be with you. She desires and pursues a relationship with you because she wants MORE of you! Isn't that a great compliment?! Your presence, attention, and interest in being with her is the "more of you" she's wanting. You matter to her and you make a huge difference in her life. She pays close attention to your attitude and corresponding actions (heart-felt?). Pursue her, engage her, and love her. When we forget how important we are to our wives, and forget that what we do and say have a tremendous impact on her, we come across as selfish and uncaring. Once that idea gets set in her mind, it can be extremely difficult to "un-set" it. We cannot allow that to happen because we then bring on the very thing we fear the most in our relationship: REJECTION! We build a lack of access to the one person who chose to be with us for the rest of our lives.

FOR WIVES ONLY:

Two of the most common phrases I've heard from husbands over the years are: "I know how to make things worse in our marriage, but I have no idea how to make things better." And: "It doesn't matter what I do; I can't please my wife." So, we end up doing nothing—that definitely sends the wrong message. You matter to your husband. That's why when he gets upset, he reacts by being defensive and/or avoidant with you (defensiveness and avoidance are two of the most common reactions men display). In many cases he is hardly indifferent to you. He loves you. You are important to him. But I'm not wanting to instill any "false hope" in you. I know your many attempts to pursue and try to engage him in a relationship, over time, has been discouraging for you.

I'm hoping to help him see, understand, and engage you differently going forward. I'm suggesting you keep an open mind and heart and try to be encouraging, and appreciative if he begins making attempts to pursue you for the relationship you've always hoped for. It is even his feeble efforts that will make the biggest difference now. If possible, try to give him a positive response. I know your marriage relationship has always been important to you.

Now about the times when women have expressed to me how much work marriage can be for them: Anne Tyler wrote: "I mean you're given all these lessons for the unimportant things—piano-playing, typing—how to balance equations, which, Lord knows, you will never have to do in normal life. But how about parenthood? Or marriage, either, come to think of it? Before you can drive a car you need a state-approved course of instruction, but driving a car is nothing, compared to living day in and day out with a husband."

I get it. Learning and doing tasks is far easier compared to trying to engage and invite your husband into the partnership (on all levels) you so want to share with him. Sometimes men are oblivious. Sometimes men are avoidant because they want to "protect their free-agent status," to do what they want. But most of the time men are afraid. Afraid you will be too demanding. Afraid you will be too critical of him. Afraid he will disappoint you—or he really will fail in the relationship. It is his responsibility to own his fear and concerns and talk to you about them. Because, if he does, you can and will do something to engage with him and work with whatever is between you in order to build a stronger relationship. This is why women feel at times that "marriage is work" for them. You are only trying to engage your husband in a talking, understanding, cooperative, supportive, loving, and close relationship. If he is not giving you a "good response" to your efforts, that can be a lot of "work." Period.

Chapter Two

Say you come into my office for counseling and you say: "My wife says I don't love her, but I do! I'm worried my marriage is going to fall apart for no good reason, and I can't prevent it!"

THIS IS A very common concern men bring into counseling. Wives feel neglected, and husbands are baffled about how their wives got such an idea, and then husbands feel unjustly accused and wives feel doubly neglected. So often it is because she doesn't see or feel that he is present or attuned to her. He is not paying attention or listening. Someone once said that for a person to suspend themselves and truly tune in and listen to another person is the greatest expression of love they can give to that person. Here's what you need to know: Your wife wants to be seen, heard, and appreciated by you. For that to happen you have to consciously, intentionally, and purposefully give her your full attention. I don't mean just look at her, but look at her so you "really see her." Consciously look at her and see the woman who loves you and chose to be with you. The woman who cares about you and does things every day to make your life better. The woman who wants to have a relationship with you, daily. Do you see her? Now open your ears, your mind, and your heart to her. Tell her your intention to listen to her stories about life, her joys, her worries, her dreams, and her fears. There are a lot of very good conversations you, as a husband, can have with her around just those five aspects of her life. To "lean in" and listen to her means you have to be purposeful in your presence with her. Not going through the motions, but bringing your presence and full attention to her. When you do engage her with your full interest and intention, don't be offended when she says: "Who are you and what did you do with my husband?" That funny response alone confirms that she is feeling your full presence and attention.

Reader: "So, now what do I do then?"

Now that you've given her your full attention and interest, you listen. Listening is the most important activity you can do in a conversation with your wife. If you don't listen, you can't have a conversation with her. If you can't have a conversation with her, you really can't have a relationship with her. And by now you know "your wife wants to have a relationship with you." That's why she worries that you're not listening to her, as was mentioned in the opening question. Listening means you suspend your thinking about your response, and your interpretation of what she is saying, while she's talking to you. You need to pay attention to what she's saying. The words she's using. The inflection in her voice as she talks. Her mood and the emotion of the content she is talking about. Look at her facial expressions. Watch her mouth and the way she says things. John Gottman says: "We need to listen to understand our spouse—not to respond to them *(2)*." In my experience, men often don't think that listening is "doing anything." To them, listening is a "passive activity." Oh, contraire. When we are really listening, we are focused, curious, working to understand and make sense of what we are hearing——it is actually a lot of work. But when we listen to our wife, it is a "work of love." And it is the most important action we can give. So, we listen to understand because when we understand our wives, our hearts open up to her and we can begin to imagine what it must be like to be in her place at the moment, as she tells us her story. This creates a moment of empathy. Empathy strengthens our bond with her, and builds closeness.

Harville Hendrix (3) is a psychologist and marriage therapist who developed what's called "Imago Therapy." "Imago Therapy" is organized around a structured process that orders and organizes couple's conversations to limit reactivity, interruptions, and "runaway arguments." His work focuses on helping couples learn about and develop ways of having better conversations. His approach is to work on couple's listening to their partner, better understanding each other, and developing empathy in their interactions.

I would add two aspects to Hendrix's work. In my experience when spouses empathize they begin to feel compassion for each other. After all, our spouse's life is not easy—they are married to us, aren't they?" As I've always said: " I married so much better than my wife did." Compassion opens us up to act with kindness toward our wife. I think of kindness as giving our wives grace, mercy, and love. Grace is a willingness to give more than might be deserved. Mercy is acting in the relationship with the knowledge that our spouse is vulnerable around us because she loves us so much. Our judgments, opinions, and actions have an impact on her. And love is the "glue" that holds us together. Love is the greatest of all human motivators. It is the most important part of human life. Period.

There are two things I want to clarify about what we're talking about now. They're both important to know and understand going forward. They are: 1. Knowing that understanding and agreement are two very different things. We work to understand our spouse first, then we talk about the level of agreement we have to work with. Then, once we know the level of agreement we have, we can talk about our plan to manage our differences. 2. When our wife tells us something, it is personal about her, not us! The first topic…the distinction between understanding and agreement. Some people think, "if you understand me, you will certainly agree with me." Not true! Harville Hendrix reminds us that we are married to an "other." Our wives are not us. She grew up in a different family, in a different place, with different experiences and perspectives. Of course, she is going to look at things and approach situations differently than we would. To add insult to injury, John Gottman reports in his studies that couples disagree (to some extent) on sixty-nine percent of the issues they deal with in their lives together **(4)**. His solution is to help couples talk through and work to understand each other better as they strive to work out their lives together. So, our goal is to work toward understanding each other, not necessarily agreeing all of the time. We can always understand our wife—agreement is less certain, and in some ways less important to the relationship.

I once worked with a couple who were in a fair amount of conflict around parenting their two children. She grew up in a family where her father was a college professor in child development.

His father was a State Highway Patrolman. They worked it out. They loved each other and their children. That had been "lost" in their arguments. And they did choose each other for their lives together.

The second thing that men need to understand (everybody, really) is that ninety percent of what comes out of your wife's (and other people's) mouth is personal about her, not you *(5)*. She is sharing her perspective and experience with you and it's an important time to be curious, and listen, and ask questions. When I first heard this, I thought it was a crazy idea, but the more I thought about it, I realized it was true; even if my name was in the sentence! I began to be curious in my own marriage, as well as talking about it in the couple's work I was doing. I found that when I believed it was personal about her, not me, I could be curious and respond to her, instead of reacting. I found couples who grew curious, instead of defensive, had better conversations, understood each other better, and actually turned the potential conflict into supportive conversations. Our response to our wife is: "You are upset. That's the most important thing right now. Please tell me more. What's going on right now? Please talk to me." You're giving your wife eye contact, and really listening to her to understand what she's saying to you. This can cause her never to say again, "You don't listen to me." She will know how much you love her because she'll feel and experience your attention and caring for her and her life.

Jill and Bruce came in to see me, reporting that their conversations "never get off the ground." Jill reported that when she talks to Bruce she can "see the look in his face drop,' and feel him slowly begin to move away from her in his attention and interest.

She reported it didn't matter what she was talking to him about—a problem, a worry, or something she was hoping for. Jill reported that she would escalate the conversation with Bruce ("you will talk to me!"), and he would then walk away.

Galvin: Bruce, is what Jill's saying accurate? Is that how it goes when she approaches you to talk?

Bruce: Yeah. That's how it usually goes.

Galvin: Bruce, can you tell me what happens to you when Jill approaches you and starts a conversation about a problem, or a worry, or something she needs?

Bruce: What do you mean, 'what happens to me?'

Galvin: What I mean is, Jill says when she's talking to you about problems, worries, or something she needs, she says she sees your face drop and she feels you relationally moving further away from her. Maybe not physically at first, but in your attention and interest in her. When that happens, I mean what is going on inside of your mind? Or your body?

Bruce: Nothing much. I just don't like it when she comes at me with her problems or things she wants from me.

Galvin: You don't like it? You don't like it when she comes at you with her problems or worries or her needs. How does it feel for you? Does it seem demanding, Jill having some expectation of you? You say Jill "comes at you" like it feels aggressive. Does it feel aggressive to you? Demanding somehow?

Bruce: I wouldn't say aggressive, per se, but it is demanding. It is like "fix this," or "I'm unhappy about that," or "get me this." It does feel aggressive at times——especially when I move away from her. Then she is yelling at me (Jill is shaking her head "NO" as she is listening to Bruce).

Jill (to Bruce): Bruce, I don't yell at you. I would never yell at you. I just don't want you to walk away from me. That's all.

Bruce (to Jill): Well, it feels like you're yelling at me. It feels like you're unhappy and somehow I'm supposed to "fix it all," "or give you whatever you want," so you feel better. I can't fix everything for you, but it sounds to me like that's what you expect from me. That's all.

Galvin (to Bruce): Bruce you say, "that's all," isn't that enough?

Bruce: I can't do it all. That's what she expects of me and I feel like she's always disappointed in me.

Galvin: Bruce, let me see if I have this right? Jill approaches you upset, worried or needing something, and what you hear Jill saying is: "Bruce, "I'm not happy and you need to fix it." Is that right? (Bruce is shaking his head "YES").

Galvin: It's hard to feel that way. It's hard to feel like a disappointment when Jill approaches you with a problem or a worry or something she needs, and all you feel is "I can't help her, and she's going to be unhappy and disappointed in me, and there is nothing I can do about it. So, when I try to get out of it, she just yells at me."

Jill: (to Bruce) I don't yell at you. I would never yell at you. I just want you to listen to me and we can talk about it. I don't expect you to "fix" things for me. I have never asked you to do anything like that, Bruce. I just don't want to feel alone in those moments.

Galvin: Jill, thanks for saying that. I think what you said is important. You said "I just want to talk with you, Bruce, so I don't feel so alone." Is that right, Jill?

Jill: Yes. That's all I'm wanting. Not to feel invisible to him and so alone.

Galvin: Bruce, can you hear Jill? Can you hear her trying to clarify what she's hoping for with you in those moments? Jill said: "Bruce, I only want you to see me, and listen to me, and be there with me. I need you when I'm worried. Not to fix me, or make me happy, just to be there with me so I'm not alone. That's why I get upset. You are not a disappointment to me; you are just not there when I need you most." (Jill is shaking her head "YES").

Galvin (to Bruce): Can you hear her? Can you hear what Jill is wanting you to know about what she needs with you? I know it's hard when she comes at you and all you can think about is what a disappointment you are to her. You can never please her. It feels impossible. But, Jill is saying the most important thing she needs in those moments is you. You are the most important person to her then. Can you hear her?

Bruce: Yes, I can hear her. (Turning to Jill): I do hear you, but this has been going on so long, it's hard for me to really believe it, but I do hear you.

Galvin: Bruce, thanks for being honest with Jill right now. The reason you get upset is because she's so important to you. What she says and does matters a lot to you. And you're right, this has been going on for way too long between you two, but what you're hearing from Jill is different from what you had come to believe about her. She is saying the same thing to you. Jill is saying: "Bruce, I do get worried, I do see problems, and I need things, but the most important thing I need is not to feel or be alone, and I come to you hoping that you will listen to me and stay with me. I don't expect you to solve all of the problems. I don't want you to ever think that. I just want for you to be there with me so I'm not alone. That's the worst part for me. Being alone." Can you hear her? Is that right, Jill?

Jill: (to Bruce) That's right. Bruce, I know we have gone around and around for way to long, and it may be hard for you to believe what I'm saying, but Galvin just said exactly how I feel and what I want. You.

Galvin (to Bruce): Can you hear that? Can you take that into your heart a little bit? Jill has been hurting, but you have been hurting too. Do you think she knows how much all of this impasse has hurt you? Do you think she understands that you move away from her to get away from your frustration and fear about feeling you're a disappointment to her? She sees it as "you don't care," but I know it's just a way to try to cope with your fear and pain around letting her down. It's so painful? Can you tell her? Can you tell her how those moments are for you?

Bruce (to Jill): It's true. What he (Galvin) says. I don't know what to do. Those feelings are hard for me and I don't know what to do. So, I try to get away. It feels bad.

Jill (to Bruce): I didn't know that. It just looked to me like you wanted to get away from me. I was afraid you were wishing maybe you weren't married to me. That's why I pursued you so hard. I didn't want you to leave me. I never want to scare you away. Bruce, I need you closer. That's all I want.

Bruce (to Jill): Galvin said it. I do become afraid that you are disappointed in me. So, your' pursuing me felt critical and aggressive..........

Jill (interrupting): Bruce, please. It wasn't aggression, really. I was desperate. It was desperation on my part. I didn't want to be left alone. Please believe me. I just got scared.

Galvin (to Bruce): Bruce, can you hear her? Can you hear her say she is afraid, too? Can you hear her say when she gets upset she just doesn't want to be alone? She wants to be with you. Jill says in those moments you are the one who can help her the most. Just being with you is what matters then to her.

Bruce (looking at Jill): Jill, I hear you. I still feel afraid that you're disappointed in me. That I'm not able to help you and I'm not helpful enough when you need something.

Jill (to Bruce): Look at me. It's my fault that I haven't been clear with you. I know now why you moved away from me. I'm sorry I've scared you. I didn't mean to. I was just afraid I was losing you. (Bruce is looking down). Look at me. I love you and just need to know you want to be with me. Ok? Galvin said it for both of us. We have been scaring the hell out of each other. I know it's hard to believe, but when I'm upset, I just need you closer. Can you do that? Please?

Bruce: That's what I want too. I didn't ever mean to make you think or feel that I didn't want to be with you. I love you, too, and never want to lose you. I'm sorry I scared you. I can work on being closer when you're upset. I just need to know you're not disappointed in me. That's all.

So, that's the direction that Jill and Bruce began to work toward in their relationship. Especially in those moments when things get tense between them. When everyone is afraid and fearing the worst. Where we become reactive instead of curious about our wife's experience. It is these moments that we, as husbands, need to take a deep breath and say to our wife: "Honey, you're upset right now, that's the most important thing; can you tell me what you're worried about?" We try to open our hearts and ears at that moment and listen. Because she is so important to us. And we remember, my wife wants to have a relationship with me.

REMEMBER:

The reason we build listening, understanding, empathy, compassion, and kindness into our marriage is because our wife's greatest fear is that she will feel and be alone in the marriage *(6)*. Many women have told me that feeling so alone in their marriage is the worst part of the relationship for them. We, as husbands, can do something about her loneliness every day. My dad was a railroad fanatic. He taught us the old railroad adage: "Stop, Look, and Listen!" I think it's a good saying for us, as husbands, to remember. We STOP and direct our full attention to our wife. We LOOK into her eyes and hold her gaze. And we LISTEN to understand her and her life. If we can practice this, she will never feel alone around us again.

CHAPTER TWO

FOR WIVES ONLY:

I wanted your husbands to know that loneliness is the last thing you want to experience in your marriage. You want to be seen, heard, and appreciated because this relationship is important to you. Your relationship is important to your husband, too. As I mentioned, his greatest fear is rejection *(7)*. Not being good enough. Being a disappointment to you. As he moves more into relationship with you, please be aware of your words and messages toward him.

Remember, you are the most important, and sometimes the only, voice speaking into his life and heart.

Chapter Three

"Why Does it seem our serious conversations derail most anytime we talk?

THERE ARE NUMEROUS reasons why couples have a hard time talking. Since this book is directed to men, let me start with the common mistakes in understanding what men need to know. First, men tend to over focus on the 'content' of the conversation they are having with their wives.

"What are we talking about?"

"What is the topic we're focusing on in this conversation?"

"What do you know about the topic and what do I know about the topic?"

In over-focusing on the "content," men often don't realize that in every conversation they have with their wives, there is another dimension that they often are either unaware of, or not paying enough attention to; and that is the dimension of "relationship." Content and relationship are both expressed in every conversation/

encounter a couple has.

The content is what the couple is talking about, and the relationship is how the couple is talking about it (relating to each other) together in the conversation. Men need to remember that their wives are always paying attention to both. Deborah Tannen *(8)*, a linguist, says: "Men talk for report (content), and women talk for rapport (relationship)." As men, we need to pay closer attention to how we are relating to our wives when we talk together. When our "relational posture" in the conversation with our wife seems disinterested, dismissive, or marginal, that is when our wife begins to feel unseen, unheard, and unappreciated by us.

Remember: she is paying close attention to what we're talking about as well as how we (you as her husband) are talking to or with her in the process.

Judith and Henry came to see me because their talking together, about anything and everything, seemed to always end in an argument, and then silent distancing.

Judith wanted Henry to talk to her more about himself and his daily experiences so she could feel like she was more a part of his life. She wanted that to be part of a daily ritual when they came together in the late afternoon after work. As part of their re-engaging, she wanted to hear his stories, thoughts, and feelings about what happened to him during the day. Henry would reply: "Look, I don't want to talk about it. Nothing really happened. It's over, anyway. What are we going to do for dinner?"

Henry didn't understand that Judith's request was not for a regurgitation/accounting of his entire day. No, she was wanting him to open himself up to her by retelling some interesting (or funny) or even life-changing story and hear about his thoughts, impressions, and feelings about it. It was far more about the relationship they shared than any content. His dismissing it sent a clear "relational" message to her and that is what she "heard" loud and clear—"I really don't care about what you want!" As men, we often don't realize that this is the message we send to our wives when we shut down conversations.

I worked with a couple, Max and Kat. Max was much like Henry in that he missed thousands of "conversational moments" with Kat in which she was asking for the "relational conversation" like Judith was. Max did understand what Kat was wanting once we talked about it. The next week the couple came in and Max reached in his shirt pocket and pulled out a small note card and showed it to me. It read: "IT'S THE RELATIONSHIP, STUPID!" Max said it was very helpful for him to carry the card around with him, especially when he and Kat talked. They both laughed and reported much longer and better conversations. Think relational.

Back to Henry and Judith. Henry wanted Judith to talk less. When he asked her how her day was, she'd start to tell him a story about a 2:00 pm meeting at work that was so upsetting. But because Deborah Tannen found in her research that "women like to build a context for the stories they are about to tell," Judith began her story about the 2:00 pm meeting with a 9:30 am email that was sent to her team. The email basically took Judith's team away from a major project they'd been working on because there was some disaster looming on another project for which they were not responsible. As Judith talks about the 9:30 am email and the impact it had on her team, Henry is rolling his eyes and asking Judith to "get to the point."

Actually, Henry said: "Judith, look, can you just tell me what happened at the two pm meeting, and if I have any questions, I'll ask." Now Judith, who had been enthusiastically sharing her story about her day, felt dismissed, negated, disrespected, and uncared for by Henry. The couple got into an argument about how uncaring he is, and what a "drama queen" she was. They spent the rest of the evening distant and avoidant of each other.

What Henry failed to realize is that for Judith, the telling of the story was not about recounting the facts (as Henry experienced it), but re-engaging their relationship and opening up their hearts and experiences to each other. She was saying, "I'm inviting you back into my life, after the day's absence, and hoping you will join me and invite me back into your life. We'll share a story or two, but more importantly, we will reconnect." It's more about the relationship and less about the content. Judith wants "more of Henry" and wishes that "he would like to have more of her," relationally. Isn't that what it's all about, really? We are sharing a relationship for life with a woman who chose to be with us and "wants more of, and with, us!" That is a very good thing, gentlemen! We need to open ourselves up to "seeing her, hearing her, and appreciating her" because she wants to be with us!

Another reason men struggle with conversations with their wives is because they don't know what their wife is looking for them to do. When she is talking to you, is she:

1. Just reporting information to you that she wants you to know? or

2. Thinking out loud and just wanting you to listen (just be a sounding board) or

3. Thinking out loud and wanting your general impressions about what she is saying? or

4. Telling you what she's thinking and wanting you to engage in a "problem solving" conversation with her? or

5. Venting her frustration, anger, or disappointment in your presence, to have a witness to her upset, experience, or dilemma? or, or, or, or?

Her reasons for talking with you could be even more numerous. What's a guy to do? How do we know what she wants? Well, I'll tell you what to do: just listen! Ninety-five percent of the time, that is all your wife wants you to do. She doesn't want you to "fix all her problems." She doesn't want you to "interpret and tell her what she really thinks or means." She doesn't want you to "repair her." She just wants you to be there, be present, and to listen to her. She doesn't want to be alone. As I mentioned before, men do not think listening is "doing anything." I'm saying rethink your' thinking on that. Listening is the most important thing you can do in your marriage. It's what she wants most from you: your attention and your ears! And by the way, there is one other thing you can do. You can tell your wife that you're going to tune in and listen to her more, but it would help you greatly if she could "preamble the conversation" by saying what it is she is wanting with you before and while you're speaking together. But the rule is: "if you don't know what to say or do—tune in and listen!"

One last notion of why conversations can be difficult for couples is the use of "triggering words and / or triggering speech." A friend of mine recently was telling me that one thing that drives her crazy with her husband is he uses the phrase "you should…." A lot. "You should do this…." "You should do that…." She says, "At times, it makes me bristle, for any number of reasons." Men often do try to "problem solve" their wife's life. I think they do this for two reasons: 1. They think they're genuinely being helpful (men like to think of themselves as having some "expertise" in knowing what to do in many circumstances); and 2. They don't want their wife to be upset because then they get "flooded" with distressing emotions and don't know what to do. I tell men that they try to "manage and contain" their wives' emotions to protect themselves from being in an emotionally distressed state themselves. We as men need to learn how to sit with our emotions and make sense of them. We need to learn how to sooth ourselves and stay present with our wives when difficult moments occur. And you need to remind yourself that your wife wants to have a relationship with you.

REMEMBER:

Husbands, there are two things we need to keep in mind at all times. First, our wives think about our relationship ten 10 times more than we do *(9)*. In every interaction, she is evaluating how the two of you are doing as a couple (Close? Distant? Adversarial? Disconnected?). She is not "trying to do this." It's just the way she sees and relates to the world. As I mentioned before, women and men see and experience the world differently. But we need to open ourselves up to engaging our wives' world through her viewpoint. We need to suspend our impatience and judgment of her style and take delight in listening to her, and watching her as she shares her life and experience with us. We also need to reciprocate, as best we can, to avoid sending her the "relational message that we really don't care."

The second thing we need to pay attention to is our tendency to be competitive in our relationship with our wife. One of the reasons men tend to be more competitive in relationships is because men tend to experience their relationships in a hierarchy (a "pecking order"). As a boy, you find out where you stand in the "male" social order on the playground with the process of two "captains" picking sides for the teams in whatever game might be played. In addition, husbands are sensitive to "not being controlled" by their wife (or anyone else), so men can quickly polarize conversations into who's "right and wrong" or "smarter than the other" or "has the better and worse ways of doing things," and the list can go on and on. Do not make your marriage into a competition (men tend to do this more than women.) Our marriage is a partnership, it is a love relationship. No self-respecting adult will accept a "second class status" in their marriage. We would never accept that for ourselves, so don't try to impose it on your wife. Instead, let's work on my client's cue and remind ourselves: "IT'S THE RELATIONSHIP, STUPID."

FOR WIVES ONLY:

You are important to your husband. As much as it seems he is "checked out" or doesn't seem to care, he does. When men get upset and are "flooded" (their heart rate goes over 100BPM), their common reaction is fight (defensiveness) or flight (avoidance). Both reactions feel negating and uncaring to you. This pattern is very frustrating, and over time can become alarming. Most women do not give up easily. As I mentioned, women want to be "heard, and seen, and appreciated" in their marriage relationship.

When they are not, they pursue their husbands. She communicates loud and clear: "You WILL hear and see me!" This is what Sue Johnson calls a "protest" against the injustice of the husband's defensiveness and avoidance. And she is right! You pursue your husband to make things right. But caught in the negative cycle, you communicate your frustration in the tone of your voice. You are "protesting" the impasse and determined for him to know how frustrated you are around his "stubbornness," and for him to know that you are "fighting for this relationship!" If possible, I suggest you pause, take a deep breath and "PREAMBLE" your intention before you start your heart-felt message. A "preamble" is a preparatory statement that intends to set a tone for what's to come. For instance, instead of picking up where you left off in your last argument (with tension and upset), you say: "Sweet cheeks, I love you and I'm so tired of us arguing and struggling to work things out, so we can be close again. I don't want to fight and I have no intention of hurting you. We obviously have some differences of perspective/opinion, but we can work to understand each other and work together. That's what I want for us." This is what John Gottman called a "softened start-up *(10)*." And men (I know you are reading this), you, too, can pause, take a deep breath, and "preamble" with your wife when things reach an impasse. You can say: "Sugar plum, I'm tired of arguing and I don't want to hurt you.......(ending with) I love you so much!"

FIRST SIXTY-SECOND TIME-OUT

Let's take a moment and breathe. How are you doing? I mentioned in the introduction that my tendency when presenting is to cover a good deal of information, hoping that something I'm saying will resonate with each reader in some way. But, I have said a lot so far. I want you to know that you don't have to try to think about all of it now. I certainly don't want you to feel overwhelmed or discouraged. If you need to, choose one or two things I've mentioned, and think about how you might want to talk to your wife about your wanting to work with her to build those things into your relationship.

All of the things I've talked about are well and good: trustworthiness; marriage is a "work of love;" see, hear, and appreciate our wife more; bringing our presence, attention, and listening ear to her; "the 90% rule;" and remembering that she is "always" thinking about what we're talking about (content), and HOW we're talking about it together (relationship). But I say these things not just for you to know and understand them, but also to encourage you to take an active role in contributing to the connection between the two of you. For your wife to see and hear and feel your interest in initiating conversation, understanding, and expressions of love and need for her in your life. These are the intentions and actions that "make her heart sing."

Your wife is not looking for you to be perfect. She only wants to know and see that you're interested and willing to invest in an active and heart-felt way, in her and your marriage. It is easy for us (men) to "get lost" in all of the things we feel responsible for and/or allow ourselves to be distracted by. This is when she feels most alone, or feels our distraction, or worse yet, feels our "not caring for her or our relationship."

So, take a pause here and take some deep breaths. Remind yourself that your wife loves you; she wants more of you in her life; and she needs you to turn toward her, make eye contact, and tell her from the bottom of your heart how much you love her, how Important she is to you, and your desire to be closer to her. Your initiating action in the direction of closeness between the two of you and sharing your need (vulnerability) for her will open her heart up to doing whatever she can to respond well in her relationship to you.

I know it seems simple, but that alone is the essence of a good marriage: mutual vulnerability (need and desire), and mutual response with deep caring and love.

The first three chapters have been focused on things you need to be aware of that you can do to better represent your love and interest in your relationship with your wife. The next three chapters are focused on the self-protective reactions we (men) do automatically to protect, or defend, ourselves from our fears. These reactions often have a negative impact on our wives and our marriage (i.e. "being a disappointment to her"). Unfortunately, these reactions are all too common, so you're in "good company" because most men react in these ways. I wanted to start with the positive things you can do first (in the first three chapters) because it is harder to "give up" doing things that don't work so well, and move yourself in a different direction (acting and expressing our true feeling and intentions), unless you have an idea or model you can begin to move toward. So, you start by expressing the positive feeling and intentions you feel toward your wife, while you begin to "manage away" the habitual reactions you have allowed yourselves to develop that totally misrepresent your true feelings and intentions, and what you're hoping for in your marriage.

Time out is up. Let's get back to the action.

Chapter Four

Boy code? What in the world is the 'boy code' and why is it important for me to know whether it impacts me and how?"

THERE ARE FOUR topics that impact men profoundly in a negative way. All four are related to each other, but each needs to be addressed separately. Two of them will be addressed in this chapter: the "boy code;" and "being controlled," and two of them in the next chapter: men's "anger" and "fear."

This question is one every young, and older, man should be wondering about. Most of us have faced the "warning" (or scorn) from other men for being too agreeable with a woman. Because "she will make you do what she wants—she will control you." Of course, the implied fear is she will "feminize" you (make you weak). The notion is that men are "strong" and women are "weak." Men often use this thinking to avoid engaging in a more intimate relationship with their wives because "if I talked with my wife about my softer, more vulnerable feelings (i.e., sad, afraid, or uncertain), she would 'fall apart' because she needs me to be strong for both of us." That is a "defensive move; blaming our wife for our not being able to do what we don't want to do in the first place!" It also reflects the prescribed behaviors of the "boy code."

The "boy code" is a set of unwritten rules and expectations about what it means to be a "real man." Basically, a "real man" (1) rejects ideas or behaviors that are feminine. The "boy code" (2) promotes men posturing as being stoic, macho, dominating, and strong. I worked with Cecil and Marie. Cecil was a strength trainer for a local professional sports team. He had muscles in places I didn't even have places. As we worked together, and I helped him talk to Marie more about his struggles and worries in their relationship, she responded well, and the couple changed their relationship to have more openness, understanding, and support for one another. At the end of our last session, Cecil got up to leave and said: "I'm going to refer my brother and his wife to you. I know they're having problems like we used to have, but let me warn you, don't tell him you're helping him to bring out his 'feminine side.' He will hit you." Husbands, being close to your wife, responding to her in a caring way, and sharing your struggles and concerns with her is not being "feminine" any more than our wife responding to us in a strong and protective way is her being "masculine." Both men and women can be open or strong at appropriate times in their marriage, in order to care for each other and the relationship. For the betterment of the relationship, let me tell you one more story. In the middle of the twentieth century, a group of scientific leaders in the fields of psychiatry and psychology got together and declared that the "mature adult human being is independent, autonomous, and self-sufficient" (sounds similar to the 'boy code'?). There was a fair amount of "push-back" from women in both fields, who protested the "absence of anything relational" in the definition. The good news is all of the social science research, as well as the brain research, over the past thirty years has proven, beyond a doubt, that human beings are "wired for connection." We were made to be in relationships. The declaration of the mental health leaders of the last century was just wishful thinking. The "boy code" pushes men in the wrong direction, and severely limits us from being part of a loving relationship. And, don't forget your wife wants to be in a relationship with you.

Why is my wife always trying to control me? Make me do what she wants?

"My wife is always trying to make me do what she wants me to do. She's always trying to control me. How do I deal with her control and manipulation without upsetting her?"

I have worked with many couples in which the "wife's controlling behavior" has been part of the presenting problem, and a concern to the husband. In some ways, this issue is tied into the "boy code" where the fear is of being controlled by a woman who will make you do what she wants and will try to "feminize" you, is to always be resisted. In fact, allowing yourself to be controlled by a woman is a direct violation of the "boy code."

And, therein lies the problem. Stay with me here as I walk through my experience and thinking about this dilemma for men (being controlled by your wife). It is tricky to get people who are "vigilant" about something (i.e., being controlled by my wife) to let their guard down enough to consider reasons why, maybe, they (the husband) have "over-thought the problem." And, maybe, they can consider seeing things differently, and respond differently, rather than react in the same-old-way. This is actually a common problem in marriages where the negative cycle has locked the couple into seeing their spouse always as a threat or a problem.

So, let me start with my clinical experience. What I know from the brain research that has been done is that "what we look for, we tend to find." So, a man who believes that his wife is controlling and manipulative (a belief that might have started earlier in his life about women), is going to look for "control and manipulation" in any interaction they have. And, in my experience, if he's looking for it, he will almost certainly find it. What is often really happening is the wife is trying to "influence" her husband into a conversation and a relationship in which they can work things out together.

*Let me just pause here for a minute and remind you that every couple has four activities they both need to be paying attention to on a daily basis: 1. Care for children; 2. Make and manage money; 3. Run a household together; and 4. Contribute to their love relationship. And there is often a myriad of other things they need to take care of together, as well. And let me remind you the "men are content with less in marital and family relationships", so they tend to under-function in terms of caring for the needs of others (i.e., expect less—do less).

So, I'm back. Men are looking for her to control and manipulate. Added to this problem, wives/mothers usually want more, and are willing to do more for their marriage and children's lives. Remember, women are vigilant about looking after the husband's and children's well-being, needs, and development. In doing so, it is not unusual for her to try to "recruit her husband" as her partner in their marriage and as parents to join her so she is not doing all of the caring alone. When men say their wife is "controlling and manipulative," he is implying she is acting in a selfish, self-serving, and self-absorbed way. She has a bad intention. I have encountered women who intend to only get their way. I'm here to tell you they are few and far between. The vast majority of women I have met are pursuing their husbands to try to get some help taking care of the things that are important to her, and by extension, them. And in my experience, the vast majority of women are acting in caring service to the people they love, for the betterment of their marriage and family life. Alicia and Elliott came in presenting a concern. This is what the conversation I hear sounds like:

Elliott (to Alicia): I'm tired of you always trying to control me. I'm not going to take it anymore.

Alicia (to Elliott): Control you? Are you kidding me? I've told you ten thousand times; I'm not trying to control you—like I ever could? You have a "ten-foot wall" erected between you and me. And there is no way for me to get to you or get your attention. Don't tell me I'm controlling! With your wall and always saying "NO!"—it's you who controls things, not me!

Galvin (to Elliott): Let me see if I've got this? You are always having to keep your guard up because you believe Alicia is always trying to get you to do what she wants you to? Is that right?

Elliott (to therapist): Yes. She has always been strong-minded. She knows what she wants, and is single-minded to go after it.

Galvin (to Elliott): Let me see if I'm hearing you correctly. Alicia has always kind of known what makes sense to her, what's important to her. And she's not afraid to try to make things happen when she sees a need. Right? Is that what you're saying?

Elliott (tentative to therapist): Right.

Galvin (to Elliott): So, it sounds like she always has a sort of plan or idea about what needs to happen in any given circumstance. She can seem clear about things or situations rather quickly, right?

Elliott (to therapist): It's uncanny at times. I'm not even sure what's going on and she has a plan like right away. Then she starts telling me what to do, and I resent it.

Galvin (to Elliott): Elliott, I get it, when she starts telling you what to do so quickly it feels totally controlling. But my experience with "truly controlling people" is that when they tell someone what to do, it's usually something that only benefits them. It's a selfish demand at someone else's expense. I'm not hearing that intention with Alicia. She's usually asking for things that help your relationship or your kids. I mean, that's what I'm hearing from all of the examples I've heard you give so far. Am I wrong?

Elliott (to therapist): No, you're right, she's not selfish—just controlling.

Galvin (to Elliott): Elliott, you happen to be married to someone who has the great disadvantage of having a quick mind and a sort of immediate problem-solving capacity. What a burden for Alicia (Elliott smiles). Then she reaches out to you, her partner, for help because she feels she can't do whatever needs to be done alone. And she comes across as demanding and controlling. What a tragedy for both of you!

Galvin (to Alicia): Alicia, are you trying to control Elliott?

*Reader: (looking at Galvin with disbelief) "Galvin, are you that naïve, or what? Here Alicia sits in a therapist's office and you ask her that question? Out loud? Really? Of course, she is going to lie about trying to control Elliott."

Galvin: Well, let me ask you, reader: "Would you lie in this situation if I had asked you the same question?"

Reader: "Don't deflect here, Galvin. This is not about me…"

Galvin: Ok, let me tell you why I asked that question. I have asked that question to hundreds of women over the years. Believe it or not, I have had a few women say "yes." At that point the conversation takes a very different direction (in those cases, the woman usually has a significant trauma history—but I digress). And all of the women who said "no" (the vast majority) were able to explain to their husbands why they acted the way they did. It was the beginning of a constructive conversation for the couple. So, can we get back to Alicia and Elliott now?

Reader: "Go right ahead."

Alicia (to Elliott): No, I'm not trying to control you. What kind of a relationship would that be for you? Or me?

And, that is the point!! If we combine the "boy code" with the fact that men are "content with less in their marriage", and women are living and breathing "relationship" and care—'til death do us part, you have the makings of a train wreck. In my experience, the vast majority of what men call "controlling and manipulative behavior" on the part of their wives, is the wife's pursuing their husband in an attempt to get him engaged in their marriage. In this negative cycle, she pursues and he resists. She feels he is not interested (or worse, doesn't care), and he begins to feel all she wants to do is make him do what she wants him to do—control him. All the wife wants is "more of him" in their relationship. She wants him to know how important he is to her. How much she needs him to come alongside of her. John Gottman called this "women trying to gain influence" with their husbands *(11).* Gottman reports from his research that the more "influence" wives can feel in their relationship with their husbands, the more satisfying (happy) the relationship is for both of them. Husbands need to never forget that your wife wants to have a relationship with you.

REMEMBER:

I love Alicia's last line. "No, I'm not trying to control you. What kind of relationship would that be for you? Or me?" This is why I'm confident when I ask women that question, the answer will be a resounding "NO." And they are perplexed with the idea that controlling their husband would somehow constitute a relationship she would want. That's not even a relationship to them, really. What women want is an engaged, attentive, supportive, reciprocal, love relationship. Wives can't "make their husbands" be in that kind of relationship. The question is, as a man, can you make yourself engage in that kind of relationship with your wife, for her sake and yours? Your wife is waiting for you.

FOR WIVES ONLY:

This is an important chapter. How did I do? What did I miss? What did I not emphasize enough? What would you add? Write down your answers to these questions and invite your husband into a conversation with you about your (and his) thoughts. Enjoy!

Chapter Five

Just a reminder that the topics of this chapter (anger and fear) are a continuation of last chapter.

Before we start, I just want to say this is the hardest chapter for me to write. The reason is because opening up to Kathy and sharing my more vulnerable feelings seems counter to my better judgment. Sometimes though, my "better judgment" isn't really better for me to act on. So, here goes......

A client came into my office and asked: "I am twenty-six years old. Recently married. I come from a long line of angry men. Both of my grandfathers were angry. My father and a number of uncles (on both sides of the family) are angry men. I have seen how their anger has damaged all of their marriages. Am I doomed to turn into an angry husband?"

It can be very helpful, as husbands and fathers, to look and pay attention to the mood problems men in our families have had over the generations. Awareness, and a decision to do something different, are the first steps in changing behavior patterns in a family. Let me talk about anger for a minute before I get into things you can do to protect yourself from being dominated by anger in your life, and damaging your marriage.

First, a man's anger can cause permanent and irreversible damage to the marriage relationship. In fact, Michael Yapko *(12)* said a man's anger is the most destructive emotion in a marriage (and family's life). Before I heard that, I would have guessed a woman's depression (wife and mom) would have been the most damaging, but when I thought about it, her unavailability, while scary, doesn't threaten immediate danger. Whereas a man's anger creates a moment in which immediate danger is possible, if not imminent. A man's anger is scary, threatening, unpredictable, and potentially physically aggressive (it already is emotionally and relationally aggressive). A man's display of anger erodes safety, security, and trust in a marital relationship. I want to be clear here, when I talk about a "man's anger," I'm referring to what is called "secondary reactive anger." This is when a man is yelling, calling names, criticizing, verbally threatening, belittling, and threatening aggressive physical contact. He is terrifying his wife.

The reason I distinguish this anger as "secondary reactive anger" is because anger is also one of seven "primary emotions" (they are: anger, fear, surprise, hurt/distress, shame, sadness/despair, and joy). We would feel anger as a primary emotion in situations like: when someone scares us, when someone takes advantage of us, and/or when someone crosses a personal boundary in our life. In these situations, we feel anger because we feel "violated" in some way. By expressing our anger openly and in conversation, we keep our feeling in the realm of "primary emotional expression" of anger. When we "fly off the handle," escalate our presentation (raise our voice), and "go after someone," then we have created the "secondary reactive expression" of anger, and the damage in the relationship begins to build.

The problem most men have is when they sense feelings of hurt, fear, sadness, or shame, they "quickly convert" these primary emotions into anger. Anger is usually bundled with all kinds of feelings, but they get ignored because the anger is so dominating. Men do this for two reasons: 1. When men feel the feelings of hurt, fear, sadness, or shame, they often get flooded with a sense of helplessness, hopelessness, and vulnerability—three emotions men don't tolerate well. Anger is an activating feeling, men much prefer to helplessness, hopelessness, and vulnerability. And 2. For men to "stay with the primary emotions," and admit to experiencing "softer feelings", they would be making themselves vulnerable to their wives (which, too, is intolerable for men—remember, many men want to get their needs met without being vulnerable). On the other hand, anger is an empowering feeling. It "gets" people's attention quickly and causes them to "back down" (if not run away). In the face of anger, people do what they have to in order to try to de-escalate the threat. So, men avoid feeling vulnerable and quickly turn softer feelings, they wish to avoid, into "secondary reactive anger" to have a more empowering experience for themselves. Unfortunately, doing this results in incalculable damage to their wives, children, and their marriages.

Before I talk about a plan going forward, I want to mention one more "anger pattern" Michael Yapko *(13)* discovered in his studies. He said people who practice this pattern actually become "anger generators" in their worlds. Basically, this is a person who cycles three things around and around in their lives, each contributing to the generation of anger. They are:

1. The person feels "entitled." They are always right and should be treated as an "exceptional" person, deserving more. Men often refer to the word "respect" as a way of demanding this entitlement. Respect and entitlement are two very different things.

2. The person is "impulsive." They give themselves permission to act out their entitlement (always justified and self-righteous).

3. The person is "externally blaming." They tell themselves that whatever happened, it is never their fault. They are always the victim of someone or something outside themselves.

When men (or women) get this cycle going, it is difficult to stop. It becomes self-sustaining. The more the person feels entitled, the more they feel justified to act out, and the more they feel persecuted by others. The more they feel victimized, the more they blame and feel entitled, and on and on it goes…. Someone once said an angry man "carries around punishment." So true.

I would like to talk about what men can do to change their perspective and behavior to end the cycle of being controlled by their anger. I am not suggesting what I'm about to put forward is for couples who have been experiencing prolonged, intense anger from the husband to his wife. I believe you, as a couple, would be best served by finding a marriage therapist in your area and setting up meetings with them to begin to de-escalate the anger, and begin to dismantle the destruction that has occurred. You will need to put into place a "safety plan" for your wife before you begin to talk about what's happened in your lives. It is the woman who decides whether she feels a safety plan is needed, or would be helpful to her, as you begin to work together.

The steps to begin to undo the problems that the anger has ushered into your marriage begins with: 1. Self-awareness. I mentioned earlier the pattern that men develop of avoiding emotion. If you cannot develop awareness of yourself and how you deal with your emotional life, anger will probably continue to dominate you and your marriage. 2. A heart-felt intention to change. Habitual behavior is not easy to turn around. You have to be willing to manage the "ups and downs" of your efforts. Not letting your frustration spill over to anger. 3. Taking one-hundred percent responsibility for your behavior in the past. If your wife could have changed things, she would have. She couldn't. You need to own your behavior and all of the fallout it has created. 4. Your commitment is to learn ways to regulate yourself, and manage your own emotions (breathing, self-soothing, taking "time-outs"). You have a plan for doing this and speaking it aloud to your wife so she can know and see what you're doing. 5. Being open and willing to hear from your wife about what it's been like for her to live with your anger. You want to hear her experience, and the pain that she has endured. And finally; 6. A commitment to yourself, and to your wife, to speak out loud the emotions you're experiencing before you "convert" them into anger. They might include:

1. Fear.
2. Hurt.
3. Shame.
4. Despair.

5. Sadness.
6. Frustration.
7. Disappointment.
8. Uncertainty.
9. Helplessness and hopelessness.

For a man to do this, he is going to have to stop his impulse to react quickly or immediately. He is going to have to learn to "sit with himself" for a moment, breathe, remember his commitment to control himself, and go inside and identify what is happening to him. Then he has to "own" and speak his feeling(s) aloud and commit to a conversation with his wife about what is happening. This is not easy. Even if you begin to make this change, things don't necessarily change quickly. If the anger has gone on for a long time (or the acute damage is significant), rebuilding trust and safety may take months, years, or maybe a lifetime. But that is not a problem, because the man's commitment to change this pattern is for his lifetime, and the lifetime of the marriage.

So, where do you start? It starts with you committing to developing the three practices that contribute to adult human maturity: 1. Taking responsibility for yourself and what you do; 2. Developing self-control, no matter the circumstances; and 3. Practicing self-discipline (making yourself do things you don't necessarily want to do). Next, you start looking at your own history of being angry with others in the world. Has this looked like the way the men in your family express anger, or has it been different? I think the third thing you do is begin to practice #6 in the list above (identifying and speaking your emotions aloud).. If you can give yourself time to "stay with your feelings," and then identify and speak them out loud to your wife, you establish a new pattern of dealing with your emotions and start a new and different conversation with your wife than you witnessed in your family growing up. Talk to her about your family history and your fears of "uncontrollable reactive anger" dominating you. Tell her of your intentions and plan to do this differently, and ask for her forgiveness, understanding, support, and help. It takes courage to face this, name it, and use it as a way to change your life now and in the future. And never forget that your wife wants to have a relationship with you!

"Am I afraid of my wife? If so, how can I tame my fear?"

I do think some men are afraid of their wives, and let me explain my thinking. For ages, the stories that men have told themselves about women are: 1. "Women are mysterious:" 2. "Men are from Mars and women are from Venus (John Gray, 1992);" 3. "Who can understand a woman?"; and 4. (and one of my former client's favorites) "women are 'crazy' and men are 'stupid.'" So, one day you meet this mysterious alien who is totally crazy and impossible to understand—to boot, and you fall in love with her and marry her ('til death do us part)! Now she has "your heart" in her hands, and she is the most important person in your whole world, and you don't have a "clue" about her or what she is up to! At this point, any thinking husband who has "connected the dots" laid out above, should be terrified out of his mind! (Ok, ok, you know I'm joking here because you've read this far in the book, and you know your wife is not a mystery, and you know she's very human, and you know she is quite understandable, and the only crazy thing she's done in her life is marry YOU—and you're glad she did!).

To be serious now, the answer is "yes, many husbands are afraid of their wives." I will tell you five ways men are afraid of their wives and what men can do to manage their worries, and feel safer and more secure in their marriages.

1. Husbands are afraid of their wife's evaluation of them. We have a couple who is a friend of ours where every year, the wife, Bridget, insists that she and her husband, Larry, sit down and evaluate their marriage over the past year, and plan for improvement in the coming year. Larry often feels clueless around what to say the problems have been, much less ideas for improvement. A few years back, things weren't going so well for them. They had a "bad year." As they discussed what happened, Larry got defensive with Bridget and said: "I know things haven't been so good between us, but I know I've been a better husband in our marriage than our friends' husbands have been in theirs." (Save yourself, Larry, throw your friends under the bus!). Bridget paused and gave the perfect response: "Hmmm. Let me see, Larry. I know those guys. That's a pretty low bar you're holding yourself up to." (Ouch—I was in that group!). So, it is important for us, as husbands, to remember that our wives are paying close attention to our relationship, and wanting to find ways to make it better. Which leads us to:

2. Husbands are afraid that things (including themselves) are never good enough for their wife. In his research, John Gottman discovered that women are always looking to "tweak" things, to make them better *(14)*. It's not that women are totally dissatisfied with things at all. They often

think of a slight improvement just to make things a little better. And since "women tend to think out loud" more than men, men hear this "dissatisfaction" and think: "Is anything ever good enough for her....?" Of course, husbands worry about this being applied to them. So, let me tell you another story. A couple I was working with had set aside a weekend to totally redo their great room in their home. Paint, window treatments, furniture, pictures, the whole "nine yards." So, when they finished late Sunday afternoon, they stood back and looked at their work. He said: "Wow, we did it! Doesn't this look great?" And she said: "I don't think the green in the throw pillows on the couch works with the green paint we used on the back wall." And he said: "Are you kidding me? After all the work we've done here? Are you never happy? Are things ever good enough for you?" They argued for the rest of the evening. When I saw them later that week, I heard the whole story and asked the husband about his comment of "nothing ever being good enough for her," and asked him if he worried that this applied to him, too? By the way, John Gottman's advice to husbands was that "'tweaking' is just the way women approach the world. It's not personal about you. It's personal about her. It's one way she deals with the world around her. Looking for little improvements, to make things better. His advice to husbands, just let it go by. She's just 'tweaking'," which leads to:

3. Husbands fear their wife is unhappy. Recently, Robin, a woman friend of ours, told me that she was sharing a sad story with her husband, Ron. She told him how unhappy hearing about this story made her feel. She reported Ron

said to her: "I just want you to be happy." Robin said he spent the rest of the day doing things just to "make me happy—which really annoyed me." Robin's question to me was: "Why does he do that? I don't want him to do things just trying to make me happy." Robin wasn't looking for happiness. She was looking for connection.

When your wife is unhappy, move in closer. "See her, hear her, appreciate her attention and sensitivity to the people and things around her." Which leads to:

4. Husbands fear that their wife will be disappointed in them. That he's "not enough" for her. He fears she is always wanting more, and he is letting her down. He fears she is judging him, and he is "coming up short." Which leads to:

5. Husbands fear their wife might leave them. For most men their wife is their best friend. For some, she is his only friend. The idea of losing her is unthinkable. He would be alone. I mean he would be alone and lost in this world. This is one reason I wrote this book because I have seen many men whose wives have left them and they were alone and lost.

That leads me to the plan going forward for husbands to deal with their fear of evaluation, their fear of never being good enough, their fear of their wife's unhappiness, their fear of being a disappointment, and their fear of losing their wife—literally. W. Clement Stone said: "Thinking will not overcome fear, but action will." So, the action is to go to your wife and talk to her about the things you fear. Together. She has fears, too. Ask her to tell you about her fears and listen. Don't worry about her being surprised that you have fears——I actually told her that you had fears a number of chapters ago. She won't be surprised. She'll probably say: "I know. I've been waiting for you to find me and talk to me about them. You know I love you. Let's talk." And don't forget your wife wants to have a relationship with you.

REMEMBER:

Face your fears. Trust your wife to give you a good response. She knows how important good responses are in a relationship. She's been wanting more of those in her relationship with you for a while. But what she really wants is for you to manage your own moods/feelings, to stop reacting, to communicate your feelings instead of going to anger, and to talk to her about your fears in your relationship with her. We all need to be loved and reassured. Don't think you don't need it——if you don't talk with her, you will really miss out, and she will be more alone!

FOR WIVES ONLY:

I have to say, this chapter really took it out of me. I hope your husbands were able to get through it and come away with some ideas to change things for himself, and for you. There is a lot of defensiveness and avoidance in anger and fear, and those two moves only make things worse for everyone. I know all you are hoping for is a chance to have an open, supportive, understanding, caring, and loving relationship. As I said to your husbands: "Don't think *you* don't need it too." (But then you already knew I said that to him, right?)

Chapter Six

"My wife complains that I am always defending myself when she brings up a problem in our marriage. I don't know what she expects me to do when she blames me for things I didn't do. What's wrong with me defending myself when she is wrong about me?"

I want to talk about two things men do habitually in their marriages: be defensive and be avoidant. In his studies, John Gottman discovered four behaviors that negatively impact marital relationships. He calls them "The Four Horsemen of the Apocalypse. They are: 1. Criticism ("you always…you never"); 2. Contempt ("putting our spouse down/shaming them"); 3. Defensiveness ("dismissing or negating what your wife is saying to or about you"); and 4. Stonewalling ("the 'silent' treatment——ghosting on steroids") *(15)*. Gottman found that these four behaviors contributed greatly to the negative cycles in couples' marriages, with contempt being the most common one leading to divorce.

So, the defensive response would be (this is what the man who asked the above question would be saying to me): "Wait a minute, you're saying I'm doing something negative. I told you my wife was wrong about what she was saying about me, I'm just setting the record straight. What's wrong with that?" There is absolutely nothing wrong with setting the record straight—if you are in a court of law where you "prove" you are right and your wife is wrong, but do you really want to go there? You are saying there is a "winner" and a "loser." But remember, we are trying to avoid "polarizing" things. You have a relationship with your wife that you want to protect from your own reactivity. You may not agree with what she is saying, but you want to respond well to her, and not damage the relationship. A good response has grace (giving her more than what you feel she "deserves" in the moment), mercy (remembering that she is vulnerable with you because you are important to her—and neither of us "gets it right" all of the time), and love (because we care about her and do not want to negate or dismiss her—ever). I know it's hard not to be defensive when she's complaining about something, and "your name is in the sentence," but your automatic move to defensiveness sends the last message you want your wife to hear and think: "I'm upset, and he (my husband) really doesn't care." Does that make sense?

There are lots of problems with "reactive defensiveness." When you are in the "reactive-defensive state of mind," you don't listen. The message it sends is: "All I hear is 'Wha, wha, wha, wha, wha, " (the sound of adults talking in Charlie Brown shows). It negates and dismisses our wife: "I'm not interested in what you're saying. You are wrong." It totally misrepresents your intentions and heart for your wife and your marriage. When we (husbands) are defensive and avoidant, we come across as disinterested and not caring. When we let these behaviors go on, it results in her seeing us as having "bad intentions" toward her. When our message to her is: "Stop complaining and leave me alone. I'm not engaging. Nothing is ever good enough for you!" (You leave her alone with nowhere to turn with her concerns about the relationship). Try to imagine her experience when you react to her defensively.

A lot of times men are hearing their wives saying: "You have bad intentions toward me." And if we have been defensive (men's first move) and then avoidant (men's second move—If they can't move away first) in the marriage, that is what she is talking about. And that is on us.

Galvin: "Yes, we might have said or done what she said (literally) in her complaint, but we didn't intend it to be mean or uncaring. That is often what men are reacting to: her experience of how she is reading our intention. But what I am suggesting is that we have to build trust, safety, and caring in our relationship with our wives, on a regular basis, so when problems arise, her questioning our intention and love for her is not part of the problem. Only we can do that, gentlemen."

Reader: "So what do I do when she is wrong? Like in my example?"

Galvin: "First of all, quit saying she's "wrong." As the old saying goes, "those are fighting words." If she told you "You're wrong" about something, I doubt your first response to her would be: "that's interesting, sweet pea, can you say more about that?" (Though it should be). No, you would do everything in your power to show her "she's wrong about you being wrong." And off the two of you would go… This is what you want to stop, right? I know it upsets you when you think she's complaining and it sounds like "you are wrong or you're the problem" somehow. That is an important moment in the relationship. That's when we purposefully make ourselves stop and listen to understand. Remember ninety percent of what comes out of your wife's mouth is about her. She is sharing her experience. Be curious. Have her explain her experience to you." Ask her questions like:

*"What happened?"

*"What did that feel like to you?"

*"What did you think about the situation? About me?"

*"Tell me more." (Always a great approach).

If you can discipline yourself to do this, all of a sudden, you are not the mean, uncaring, defensive, and insensitive husband she was complaining about. In fact, if you can tell her you love her, and you never want to hurt her, and whenever she thinks or feels something negative about you, you want her to tell you (an invitation to be close) so you can "set the record straight." I believe, if you are able to do this, you will cease to be the "uncaring suspect" in the marriage. That is what you fear she's come to see you as. We, husbands, need to pay attention to and "catch the automatic defensiveness" (a very bad habit, indeed) that has taken over our first response to our wives. Defensiveness is probably the most common reaction men exercise in their relationship with their wives. It is based in fear. We are afraid she is unhappy with us. We are afraid she sees us as hurtful and uncaring toward her and our marriage. In those moments we need to be aware of our reactiveness, and try to remain close and curious about her hurt and upset.

"Ok, that was defensiveness, what about avoidance? What's that about?"

Ok, avoidance. Susan Johnson says "Avoidance is a terrible relational strategy" *(16)*. You've heard of "fight or flight"? Two reactions human beings have when they feel threatened. Think of "defensiveness" as fight, and "avoidance" as flight. I believe a lot of times husbands avoid their wives because things aren't going well in the relationship, and "they (men) believe all they know is how to make things worse, but they don't know how to make things better," so they avoid her. The distance may seem to "solve the problem" (no contact—no conflict), but remember: what do women fear the most in their marriages? Loneliness.

Avoidance leaves your wife feeling alone. Avoidance says: "I'm not here for you." "You can come and find me in the office, or the basement, or the garage, but I won't engage you. I'll tell you I'm busy; I don't have time; or I don't want to talk." What in the relationship communication do you think she hears? Is that the message you want her to believe about you as her husband?

I worked with a woman and her two young adult sons. They had recently moved to St. Louis to be closer to her aging parents. They had lived in Montana where her husband was a professional tracker/hunting guide. He primarily took out-of-town groups out into the mountains to hunt "big game." By their report he was much in demand in the industry. She reported the couple had had marital problems from the beginning of the marriage. She reported her husband would be gone for days or weeks at a time, working. She never knew his schedule. He had an office in a town nearby where he had a bed, and often slept there. The two boys called him "the shadow" at home because he was rarely there, and when he was, they often didn't see him much. The mom reported she would "track him down" (pun intended) from time to time to try to get him to engage more around the marriage and family life, but he would tell her he was too busy working.

I know you say, "I'm not that bad!" And I admit this case is extreme, but a little avoidance goes a long way. When you couple defensiveness (fight) with avoidance (flight), as your predominant relational strategies, the message you send to your wife is loud and clear: "leave me alone, I really don't care about you!" Don't forget your wife wants to have a relationship with you!

REMEMBER:

Defensiveness and avoidance may be constant companions of yours, but they are no friends of yours! Ditch them as soon as you can! The reason we "hang out with these two" is because we get afraid when our wives get upset with us. We don't know what to do. She seems inconsolable to us at that moment, so we automatically react to "shut down the conversation." Fight or flight does that. "Fight or Flight" moves us to escalate or disengage in the moment. It is because we are afraid. We are afraid of her judgment of us. We are afraid of her unhappiness with us. We are afraid of her being angry with, or controlling, us. We are afraid "we will never please her" or "we will never be good enough." When we "ditch" defensiveness and avoidance, and get curious, we face the fear we have of our wives, and engage her in what she hopes for the most: a relationship! Yes, we can be relational and caring in the face of our own fear. As Betty Carter once told a male client: "No one ever died engaging difficult feelings

(17)." Our wife does not want to scare us, or hurt us. She wants us closer. That is reassuring and terrifying (a "double-feel"). Stay with the reassuring part!

FOR WIVES ONLY:

As I mentioned, men are defensive and avoidant because they are afraid. They feel threatened. I know it is hard to believe your husband might be afraid of you ("sounds like another excuse to me, Galvin. Are you thinking this is my fault? Nice try?" Right??). But it is true. He doesn't want you to be upset or angry with him. Men pay close attention to their wife's moods and voice tone. Of course, being defensive and avoidant contributes greatly to your feeling "unseen, unheard, and unappreciated." It becomes a vicious, negative cycle that I'm hoping your husband can see and do his part to stop, help turn it around, and build a more positive relationship with you. I know at times your husband seems oblivious, but he is aware of you and worries that you may never be happy with him, or that he's not good enough , or a disappointment to you. If possible, show him some grace (more than he deserves), mercy (remembering he is vulnerable with you), and love (he loves you, too) as he struggles to bring himself more into his relationship with you.

SECOND SIXTY-SECOND TIME OUT

Let's stop and breathe again. Let's just slow things down for a minute. How are you doing? I know I'm "speeding right along." Guilty as charged. Once more, I just want you to sit for a moment with yourself and not let the things I've talked about in the last three chapters overwhelm you. I want you to know that you are not alone in paying attention to and trying to manage the ways you cope with, and react to your fear of your wife's "criticism and disappointment" in you. I know I react that way when I think Kathy is disappointed in me. Most of the men I have worked with react that way. You are in "good company"—though our wives may say "not so good company." Ha! The reason you react to her is because she is so important to you. What she thinks and says and does matters to you. That is why you react defensively, in anger, and move toward avoidance. We all do these things. We want to feel safe. We don't know what to do in those moments. We are afraid.

I know when I started to pay attention to how often I would react defensively to Kathy, I was astounded. Just about always! I had developed a "defensive posture" toward her. She could feel it and hear it. It was because I was sensitive to feeling criticized and rejected by her. I lived "on guard to looking for negativity" from her. That's when I started talking to myself: "Hey Galvin, why are you defending yourself all of the time?" "Do you have something to be defensive about?" "If you don't have anything to be defensive about, why don't you just stop and listen to what Kathy is saying?" "Remember ninety percent of what comes out of her mouth is personal about her, not you, nitwit. Maybe you should follow your own advice and be curious?" "What is she wanting you to hear and understand?" Once I did that, I realized she was not wanting to be critical of me. She was reacting to my "defensive posture and attitude," worried I wasn't interested in her anymore. My point is, it required me to start paying attention to myself for a while to "catch my reaction" (defensive, angry, avoidant) to her and begin to minimize and contain it away from our relationship. I may be a fast talker, but I am a slow learner!

All I'm saying is you need to start paying closer attention to yourself in relationship with your wife. You need to own your fears and concerns and talk to her about both of them. She will give you a good response if you own them. Your wife wants to be helpful in your relationship. She wants to matter to you, too. She wants to make a difference in your life everyday—she wants to be a difference. That is the point of being married. You are there for each other. Life is not easy. You as a couple will face challenges and problems you can't predict or control. The one thing you can control is whether or not you, as a couple, face them alone or together. And often, gentlemen, you control the distance or connection between you both more than she does. If you asked your wife if she would like you to be closer and more available to her, what do you think she would say? I'm not a betting man, but the "over/under" on that bet would be a "no brainer" to me.

The next four chapters are more "topical." Forgiveness, repair, building a stronger connection, husbands and wives and problem talk, and the three intimacies (yes, sex is one of them). It is ok to re-read any chapters you might want to. As I have said, look for things that resonate with you and stop and have a conversation with your wife about whatever that might be; what you think about it; what she thinks about it; and how the two of you might want to incorporate it into your life together. Take a few deep breaths. You are doing great.

Our time out is up. Let's get back to the action!

Chapter Seven

"I said I was sorry, why doesn't she believe me?"

Recently another man said to me: "It always seems when my wife and I have a problem, or an argument, it's always me that has to apologize first. Why is that? Does she not think she is part of the problem in our marriage, too?" A triple whammy.' The "trifecta" of disaster in the husband's eyes: 1. She makes me say "I'm sorry" first; 2. Then she doesn't believe me when I say "I'm sorry;" and 3. She doesn't think she is part of the problem in our marriage. "She, She, She......." Can you hear yourself? Ok, gentlemen, it's time to let it go and stop focusing on your wife and start focusing on YOU. Let's focus on what you can do to effectively repair impasses and injuries in your marriage.

Apologies in a marriage are very important. But before we get to talking about "the apology," let me set the perspective about: 1. how we understand ourselves (the human condition), in order to understand why apologies are important, and 2. why your wife might think it's important to hear your apology first.

We all long for someone to love us and be there for us, in spite of our quirkiness and flaws. We all long for that lover to open their heart to us, trusting us to understand them, love them, and want to be with them; even knowing their secrets and fears. We all long for intimacy to be "known and loved." But, there is a catch: "You can't be intimate in a marriage without being vulnerable," and none of us want to be vulnerable, especially men. Intimacy has at its core an openness to being "known" by our loved one, and probably being able to be hurt by that same person. Singer/songwriter, Billy Joel wrote a song titled, "And So It Goes." One line in the song says: "And you can have this heart to break." How romantic, right? That is what falling in love looks like. It compels us to open our heart and soul to another person, and trust that their love for us will protect us (be stronger than) from any harm that may come in the relationship. Let me spell out the challenges to this wonderful idea ("my love will be stronger than any harm I might bring to you") as people enter marriage.

Psychologist, Rick Hanson *(18)*, reports from his studies that all human beings have a "negativity bias" built right into their brains. Hanson reports that two-thirds of the neurons in our amygdala (the emotional center of our brains) are oriented to "danger." This makes us "vigilant to trouble in our environment." Our brains are designed to keep us safe (survival). Hanson notes that people come into marriages with limits and vulnerabilities—baggage from their prior life and relationships. We all bring personal and interpersonal challenges, along with limited resources into our marriage.

If that is not enough, another psychologist, Harville Hendrix *(19)* reminds us that our spouse is not us. What? We are not married to ourselves. We are married to an "Other." Our spouse has had a very different life experience growing up than we did, and they bring that difference with them into the relationship. I know you're thinking "this is not good!" However, actually, it is very good for us. What is good about it is that our spouse becomes a great "reality tester for us." They help us to see the world from a whole different point of view. They help us learn how to negotiate, compromise, tolerate, give and receive, and grow up; all in the context of a love relationship. All of this is why a colleague of mine said: "Every married couple needs to have grief counseling at their first anniversary." "This is not what I 'signed up for' or expected." But if we stay the course, it turns out so much better than what we ever thought, as we grow together. In his book, *Canoeing the Mountains*, Tod Bolsinger's advice to leaders: "Stay Calm, Stay Connected, and Stay the Course **(20)**." This is a very good mantra for married couples to remember as they navigate the challenging rapids of their life together.

So, to summarize, we enter into the most complicated of all human relationships with a "limited" person whose brain is wired to detect negativity in others (read: us), in a difficult and challenging world, while bringing problems with them and having limited resources, and their "Otherness." And we fall in love with them and say: "You can have this heart to break." This is why repair and forgiveness are so important and necessary in a marriage. We all need to see that our apology is the expression of love that is greater than the problems we face. When we apologize, love wins!

Now let me pass on my experience as to why your wife wants you to initiate the apology in your marriage. It starts with a story.

In Parade Magazine a while back, the advice columnist, Marilyn Van Sant (a profoundly intelligent person) was asked a question by a woman writing in: "Marilyn, my husband and I have been having an argument. He says that men built the world, and I say that men and women built the world together. What do you say, Marilyn?"

Marilyn wrote back: "Honey, it is men who have built the world, but it's women who have civilized it!" Marilyn is a genius, because women have civilized the world by shifting it from being about power and control (men's default move) to relationship, socialization, and collaboration. On the level of marriage, it boils down to nine words: "Your wife wants to have a relationship with you." One pattern I've seen in my practice experience is that early on in marriage (and relationships), women tend to apologize sooner and more often than their husbands. They do this because it's relational and that's what women do because they "live in relationship." As the marriage progresses, and the husband does not respond in kind when there is trouble (that is, his acknowledging his part in her feeling hurt and upset, too), she begins to back away because she feels he is not seeing or acknowledging his responsibility to being in the relationship with her (read: responsiveness to her hurt in the exchange). As I mentioned, men tend to see marriage as "transactional," and things that happen as "events," not necessarily connected to all other "events." Women tend to see relational patterns. That is why she brings up exchanges from the past (not to "pile on," but to say: "can't you see, there is a problematic relational pattern here?"). So, here is my theory on why your wife waits for you to approach her with an apology (please feel free to check it out with her): "thinking relationally, she used to apologize first and more often to show her responding to your upset, relationally." When you didn't respond in kind, she didn't know if you saw or knew how upsetting it was for her when you argued, so she is waiting to see if you are: 1. Paying attention to what is going on between you two ("It's the relationship, stupid!"); 2. If you care about her, and not just winning the argument; and 3. Are willing to move toward her and repair and restore the relationship with her? Remember, men over-focus on the content and often miss the relational side of the interaction.

Let's move on to the apology itself now. It's not easy or pleasant to say those two words that could make all of the difference in a difficult situation: "I'm sorry." It can be your pride (read: stubbornness), or not being in control. Or you may see the relationship as a power game and saying "I'm sorry" is losing ground in the relationship struggle. This can block men from being able to say it. Saying "I'm sorry" makes us vulnerable. So often men think two things: 1. If I say "I'm sorry" that means I'm taking full responsibility for all of the problems or mess that have happened here; and/or 2. If I say "I'm sorry" it will just be the "beginning of all the things I will be forced to say I'm sorry for" (then the only thing I really will be sorry for is that I ever said "I'm sorry" in the first place!). Yikes! When I have heard men say about their wives: "she will make me" in sessions, I usually respond: "Really, like your wife can 'make you' do anything? If she could do that, I never would have met you. She would make you do all of the things that she knows will make you a better man, and make your marriage better, and you would be the happiest man on the planet! But we couldn't have that, could we?" He usually smirks, and she laughs.

Our marriage is a personal relationship. It is a love relationship. It needs to be nurtured and protected. It is not about power (I have seen many marriages where "power" is the dynamic between the couple. The marriage is not easy or pleasant). It is about love, and love is about giving of ourselves first and foremost. As husbands, it's about thinking of our wives before we think about ourselves. So, in that vein, let me suggest another meaning for the word "I'm sorry." One that fits better the personal, intimate, caring, love relationship that we want to be in. The idea comes from the Spanish word for "I'm sorry:" Lo Siento. It means "I feel……" I feel your pain. I feel your hurt. I feel your upset. I feel YOU. When we think of an apology with this meaning, the idea of power, or coercion, or manipulation, or a "mechanical apology," mouthing the words disappears. Here is what that would sound like:

*"We can figure out later what happened in our conversation. Right now, I can see that you're upset and that is the most important thing to me. Can we talk? Tell me what's happening for you? I am so sorry. I'm right here. Please tell me."

"I feel" requires attunement. Attunement comes from intentional attention and interest directed at our wives. Attunement, attention, and interest comes from our hearts. That is what our wives want to feel from us. They want to know that our hearts are in our relationship with them: for better or worse, in good times and hard times, as long as we both shall live.

Tessa and Taylor came in to see me regarding their struggle to manage her parents. It's not unusual for couples to have problems or difficulties with people or things (i.e., activities) outside of their relationship. Tessa grew up in a very under-organized family.

Her parents neglected most everything in the house, including their children. Projects were rarely started, and never finished. This was a great source of pain and embarrassment for Tessa. She would never have any friends over because of the constant chaos and mess. Taylor was one of three boys in a highly organized and functioning family. Being competent, and seen as such, was the value for all three boys. Tessa and Taylor had been married for twelve years and had two school-aged children. The problem was Tessa's parents. They lived two hours away in a more rural area. They would "drop in unannounced" from time to time, expecting everyone to drop everything and entertain them ("after we travelled all this way?!"). The "straw that broke the camel's back" occurred during the prior weekend when Tessa and Taylor had set aside that time to do a home project (a total makeover) in the kid's bedrooms. They had been planning this for over a month, and moved kids' activities and theirs in order to accomplish it in one weekend. Her parents showed up unannounced early on that Saturday morning. Her father decided he wanted to go to a baseball game downtown. The game started at 12:15 p.m. The parents hadn't eaten breakfast yet. And Tessa's mother was refusing to go to the game. Instead, she told her husband that Taylor would go to the game with him and she would stay home and be with Tessa and the kids. Tessa explained to her parents they already had plans, but Tessa's mother insisted she would help Tessa with the project if Taylor would go to the game in her place. She convinced Tessa of the plan (even though Tessa, deep down, knew better), and her mother was yammering on Taylor, who eventually agreed.

*Let me stop right here and say something important. Couples should never negotiate, with each other, or make decisions that are "their decisions to make as a couple" in the presence of anyone else (i.e., parents, the Pope, the President, anyone). Every "couple's decision" is made in private, away from everyone else and other's influence. Period. Making their couple and family decisions in private without the influence of anyone else is the new rule Tessa and Taylor learned the hard way, but now they say "no more!" Neither of them wanted the outcome her parents had brought to them.

Of course, the project didn't happen. The baseball game had a three-hour rain delay, and Taylor and his father-in-law didn't get back home until 8:00 pm, exhausted. Claiming it was too late to drive back home, Tessa's parents stayed overnight, slept in late on Sunday, and by the time they left it was two in the afternoon. The next week Taylor had to work late a couple of evenings, and the household fell apart. In her frustration and anger, Tessa yelled at Taylor for "being just like her parents" and not caring about getting anything done. And she did it in front of the kids. Taylor was shocked and very hurt by this attack. They continued arguing until they came into my office. After their talking about their dilemma with her parents, we came around to Taylor telling Tessa how hurt and upset he was that she said what she said about him, and in front of the kids.

Tessa: I said I was sorry. You could have said "no" to my mother. You know how hard it is for me to do that.

Taylor: You had already said "yes" to your mother. I was there, what was I going to say at that point? I didn't even want to go to the game in the first place. Don't blame me for this. You said "yes" first.

Galvin (to Tessa): I'm assuming you would like to resolve this with Taylor. I know you two have done nothing but go around and around about it. Is that right?

Tessa: Yes. I would like to resolve this with him. And I already apologized once.

Galvin: Ok, then. It's important that you stop being defensive and stop making excuses about how you handled this, and focus on what Taylor is saying to you. Taylor, can you please tell Tessa what happened to you when she said, "you were just like her parents and you didn't care about getting anything done with the house"?

Taylor: Tessa, there is a part of me that can't believe you would ever say what you did to me. I mean, I have been nothing but… (I interrupt)

Galvin: Taylor, I'm going to stop you here, I don't know if you heard me clearly, and maybe I wasn't clear about what I was asking, so let me start again. Can you please tell Tessa what happened to you in the moment when she said, "You are just like my parents and you don't care about getting anything done in the house"? Stay with me here. Just in that moment what were you feeling?

Taylor (pausing to think): I was devastated. I was shocked. I couldn't believe what I was hearing. I was humiliated, too, in front of the kids. They know what their grandparents are like. They have heard the stories like…(I interrupt)

Galvin: Ok. OK. That's good, Taylor. Tessa, I know you were

looking at him when he just said he was devastated. What happened to you when he said that?

Tessa (tears forming in her eyes): That shocked me to hear him say that word. I didn't know that's how he felt. It's terrible. I would never want to hurt him like that. He's right. He has been a great partner to me, and my 'issues' around getting things done. I'm glad he said it, but I know it really hurt him that I said it in front of the kids. I know what it's like to feel humiliated. (turning to Taylor) I never want to humiliate you, ever. (Softer) Taylor, I am so sorry for what I said and did. I wish I could take it back. I never meant to hurt you. I know my apologies before haven't been very sincere, but looking at you now and hearing you tell me the impact of what I said, I want you to know how truly sorry I am. Please forgive me.

Taylor (reaching for her): Thank you. It really scared me when we just kept fighting about it. I didn't know what to do. I love you and I have been feeling how much I need you to love me back. It's been a very difficult week. And I do accept your apology. Can you talk to the kids, too, please?

Tessa (rubbing his arm): I love you, too. And I am so sorry. I will apologize in front of the kids tonight to make it right with them, too.

Taylor: Thank you. I would appreciate that.

Galvin: Is there any more, Taylor? Any more stuff here you need to talk about?

Taylor: No, that really makes a difference. I think we're good.

Galvin: Tessa, how about you? Is there any more you want to say? Or anything more you need to hear from Taylor?

Tessa (looking at Taylor): It really makes a difference when you tell me how much you love me and how much I matter to you. You know I grew up not feeling very important. I need you to remind me more often if you can. I feel so secure when you do that.

Taylor: I love telling you that. I know you didn't hear or feel how important you are, or how much you're loved, growing up. I will definitely remind you more often what a difference you make in my life.

So, you can see that when Taylor was able to tell Tessa what really happened to him in that moment, Tessa could attune and empathize with him. Taylor softened and shared more about how important she was to him (how vulnerable he is); giving Tessa more safety to take responsibility for what she did; hearing this, Taylor was able to ask for more of what he needed: the kids' esteem, and receiving a good response. The couple has successfully navigated a difficult time in their relationship and has learned how to stay focused on each other to resolve an impasse together. By doing this, the injuring spouse abandons defensiveness, and restores love and safety. The hurt spouse abandons anger, and restores openness and hope.

We husbands need to remind ourselves that marriage is an intimate love relationship. The reason we are vulnerable to each other is because we're so important to each other. We matter. We make a difference. We have impact in things we do and speak. We need to communicate to our wives how much we want to support, encourage, and care for them. There are infinite ways to be misunderstood. There are numerous ways we can upset our wives. But today we make a pledge to ourselves to communicate to her that "our love will be stronger" than our clumsiness, selfishness, inattention, and stubbornness (I'm sorry guys, I had to say it). And when "trouble calls," my attitude to my wife will be attunement and "Lo Siento"—I'm right here and I care. And I won't forget my wife wants to have a relationship with me.

REMEMBER:

We are limited people in a difficult world. We are married to an "Other," who grew up very differently than we did. Our brains are oriented to "watch out for trouble" (and the old saying "what we look for, we tend to find" is true). Our wife is trying to induct us into a real, every day, engaged relationship (instead of compartmentalizing and dissociating). And when things are difficult, "what we focus on, we amplify" (Another way our brain can either protect us or make trouble for us). With all of those challenges, we as husbands need to stay humble and open, at the same time, to the wonderful things our wives wish for us in life. We need to remember how important she is to us. We don't want to hurt her or leave her feeling alone. We have a huge impact on her (more than we might ever know). So, when she is hurt by us or upset with us, the only move is toward her (unless she says otherwise) to listen, tune in, understand, empathize, be compassionate and kind, and apologize to her when needed because that tells her: when you hurt, I hurt! That is love.

FOR WIVES ONLY:

Ok. Ok. I know what's coming! I hear YOU! Why in the world would you write a book for my husband and have the wife be the one to apologize in it? What were you thinking? Those are good questions! Ok. Next question, please? Just kidding. I have two very good answers to those two very good questions. The first is that if I wrote the transcript where I was able to get the man to apologize (and I have helped many men get there), I would have had to cover about twenty pages for the transcript. "No, Doug, let's go back again……..No, Doug, let's go back again…….No, Doug, maybe I didn't say it as clearly as I could have (for the 47th time)………….." And if I had written the conversation between Tessa and Taylor and switched their roles, no one on the planet would have believed that Taylor could respond that well, that quickly. So, to make the point (and protect what integrity I may have remaining in this book) I decided to tell the real story. My second reason is that men can learn a lot from women about relationships (ok, don't tell your husbands I said that—what's said in "WIVES ONLY," stays in "WIVES ONLY." Right?!)

When men tell me, "My dad wasn't a very good husband, so how could I be a good husband with a dad like that?" Or, "my dad was a terrible father, how could I ever be a top-quality dad?" I look at these men and ask: "What about your mom, was she a good wife? Was she a good mother?" I then go into what these men experienced and observed about their mother as a wife and mother. I ask them why they can't say and do things that they admired in their moms. For most men, the idea never occurred to them. For many of us, we grew up in a home with two parents. For others of us, we had two parents, but they didn't live together. Regardless, most of us had two parents in our lives from whom we could learn about relationships. When we grow up with two parents, why don't we learn from either of them? So, these men start describing with some detail what their mothers said and did (as mothers and wives) that left a positive impression on them, and I ask: "Can you do that?" "Can you say that?" And when I see couples and the husband is telling me he's not very good at relationships, I ask him: "Do you wish you could be better?" Most say "YES." Then I say: "This is your lucky day because I think you're married to someone who actually has a lot of ideas about what makes a relationship good. Would you like to meet her and maybe we can get started on a conversation about the things you'd like to work on? Maybe get her ideas?!" I know at times it's difficult, but try to: "Stay calm, stay connected, and stay the course."

Chapter Eight

"How do I rebuild trust after a terrible mistake"?
Or years of "getting it wrong"?

A CLIENT CAME to me and reported: "About two years ago I had an affair. I ended the affair and told my wife. I regret what I did and we have been rebuilding our relationship. What kinds of things do I need to be paying attention to and work on from my side? This has been very painful for both of us."

A spousal affair is a nightmare for the impacted spouse. It destroys so many things in their world: their trust; their sense of security; their belief in their spouse; their belief in their marriage story; their reality testing; their belief in their life story; their faith in God; and worst of all, a basic trust in themselves *(21)*. They are haunted by questions like:

*"How did I not see this happening?"

*"What have I done to deserve this (self-blame)?"

*"How can I trust my spouse ever again?"

They enter into the world of 'What I don't know can hurt me.'

*"How can I find out what I don't know, so I can feel safe again?"

The offending spouse's job going forward is to do everything he can to restore safety and sanity for his wife in that relationship (I'm speaking to the husband here because that is who asked the question). You need to speak your remorse until she tells you that you don't need to speak it anymore. Couples can and do "heal" from an affair. They can restore "safety and trust" to their relationship. Genuine forgiveness can be offered and accepted, but the fact that the affair happened will never be forgotten. It is a devastating event in any marriage.

*"Honey, I want to tell you how sorry I am for what I've done to us. I will tell you as many times as you need to hear it. What I'm saying comes from the bottom of my heart. I wish I could go back and undo what I did. I'm so sorry. And I will say it until you tell me 'It is ok not to.'"

You need to take one hundred percent responsibility for the choice you made. Your wife wasn't asked or informed of your decision, so she has no part in choosing what you did (except to be devastated). Sometimes, a spouse may blame the affair on "problems in the marriage." The truth is: lots of marriages have problems, but in those circumstances, neither spouse chooses to pursue an affair. So, it is a relational mistake for any spouse, who has chosen to have an affair, to somehow implicate their partner in their choice.

It's important for you to be "accountable" to her. Open up your calendar and all the devices you can. Open up your whole life, so she can see what you're doing all of the time. You lost sight of yourself and your marriage. The only way to restore those two things is for you to completely reopen your life and invite your wife back in. This is difficult for men. They often feel "supervised, spied on, controlled, and on lock-down." All of those things are "true" if your view is only from your perspective. And of course, we know that when you pursued the affair, all you were thinking about was yourself (where were the thoughts of your wife and the fact you were married and had a commitment to her?) That is the course you need to reverse. You are now thinking of her and what she needs from you to restore trust. Repairing the affair cannot be about you. It is all about what you've done. When you shatter trust, you forfeit your right to privacy until you can restore that trust, unless you have no regard for the marriage.

*Privacy is information you know and keep to yourself because the information itself doesn't hurt or compromise anyone else's life. Privacy does not cause harm to others.

*Secrecy is knowing and keeping information that would negatively impact another person's life, and they are unaware of it (i.e., an affair in their marriage). Secrecy causes harm to others.

You have "taught" your wife that "what she doesn't know will hurt her (devastate)". Now you need to "flood" her with as much information as she needs to restore her sanity, security, and safety. She needs safety from you; you need hope from her so that a solid, loving relationship can be restored.

I worked with a couple in which the husband had had an affair. His wife reported in a session that she had had a dream shortly after the disclosure. They lived on a rural property with a house, a barn, and a workshop for her architectural business. In her dream, a tornado hit their property. It tore up all of the land, damaged the barn and workshop, but totally destroyed the house down to the foundation. What an image. It struck the husband in a way that clarified the impact of the affair on her. If you have had an affair, don't minimize the damage you've done. Your wife decides the damage and you respond to restore and rebuild that damage.

"So, when we're trying to build in a more secure and solid foundation to our marriage, what should we be paying attention to? What is that foundation we wish to restore? What should I be doing to rebuild with her?"

The foundation of a marriage is made up of three components: 1. Commitment; 2. Safety/protection; and 3. Love. These are the things that every married couple needs to pay attention to and talk about on a daily basis. No one takes care of a marriage except the two people in it. And our culture is not a friendly environment for marriages. Sadly, in this case it took an affair to get the couple focused on developing their relationship. Many couples I've worked with who have survived an affair, work harder post-affair on these three areas, daily, than couples who have not faced that crisis. Of course, on one level it makes perfect sense because the couple that has faced being "on the edge of the cliff (surviving an affair)," and realizing the importance of their marriage, is going to focus on restoring their commitment, protect the relationship, and work to restore love and safety. And they are going to do this consciously, intentionally, and purposefully daily.

Usually, in rebuilding, we start with Commitment. Here is what commitment sounds like:

*"I'm glad we're together and I'm married to you."

*"We have a full-blown catastrophe (kids, mortgage, jobs, chores, bills in-laws, outlaws, dogs, cats, etc.) on our hands, and I wouldn't want to go through this with anyone but YOU!"

*"I'm glad we're growing up together, and I'm looking forward to growing old with YOU!"

These are the messages of commitment. When we say these words we are reaffirming our pledge of trust and commitment to our wives. We are saying "you are not alone." We are saying "I see you; I hear you; I appreciate you." And because we are fickle and vulnerable, we need to remind OURSELVES of our commitment. The best way to do this is to speak it out loud to our wives so she can hear it and feel it, often. And we say it aloud so we can hear it and feel it ourselves, and live our commitment, protection, and love for our wife daily.

Words of PROTECTION and SAFETY sound like this:

*"I'm glad we're together and I won't let anyone or anything get between us."

*"I know you worry at times about losing me—losing us—but I want you to know that I only want to be with you. No one else."

*"What can I do today to show you how important you are to me, and how important it is that you're feeling safe and secure in our relationship?"

Our wife needs to know she is first in our lives, and our taking care of the relationship is the strongest line of defense protecting our marriage. As I've said, if the couple doesn't protect and nurture their marriage, no one else will. It is important for married couples to "speak into each other's lives" on a regular basis. Research shows that if a couple does not have loving contact in their relationship, after forty-eight (48) hours **(22)** they begin to feel alone and wonder if their spouse has lost interest in them. For women, the contact is more the verbal/emotional connection. For men, it is more their sexual relationship. Safety is important. It is near impossible to give all of yourself and love someone you don't feel safe with. Let me remind you that there are more ways to breach safety in your marriage relationship, other than an affair. In his book, *What Makes Love Last?*, John Gottman **(23)** devotes one chapter to the ten areas of betrayal (other than a sexual affair) that damage a sense of safety and trust in a relationship. They are: 1. Conditional commitment; 2. A non-sexual affair; 3. Lying; 4. Forging a coalition against your partner; 5. Absenteeism or coldness; 6. Withdrawal of sexual interest; 7. Disrespect; 8. Unfairness; 9. Selfishness; and 10. Breaking promises. The list is not comprehensive, but helps us to understand that safety and trust issues can be physical, emotional, cognitive, spiritual, and relational. Protecting each other in the marriage communicates to the outside world the intent of both partners to stand together and provide the support and loyalty needed to withstand the threats and challenges of the "outside world." And last but not least: LOVE. Love is the experience we have when we allow ourselves to "totally fall into" a relationship where we want to give a commitment of ourselves, and the protection that goes with it, to another person who wishes to reciprocate for us. It means giving ourselves over to our wife, feeling total freedom to lose ourselves in the security of her love for us. The words of love sound like:

*"I love you!"

*"As our relationship matures, I find myself loving you in ways I couldn't have imagined before." (Make a list)

*"Do you know what I love most about us being together?" (Make a longer list).

*"Do you know what I love about you the most?" (Make the longest list).

In the words of the poet, Elizabeth Barrett Browning: "How do I love thee, let me count the ways." Love is at the core of a life-long, stable marital relationship. Love is interest, attraction, curiosity, motivation, affection, sexual chemistry, and the list goes on and on. Webster uses words like: fondness, tender feelings, devotion, passion, and sexual attraction. Love also has a component of willingness to give, change, and sacrifice for another. Love is both simple and complicated at the same time. Love is strong and fragile at the same time. Love is the greatest of all human motivators. Love is the reason people want to commit and protect a loved one for a lifetime. At the same time, love can wax and wane——like cycles of the moon (how romantic is that?) Couples need to stay attuned to the "ebb and flow" of their experience, as well as their partner's, in order to better respond to and initiate connection around their spouse's needs.

Will and Stacy were struggling in expressing and experiencing the security, safety, and love in their marriage. They were both frustrated by the long periods of time during which they were avoiding each other in the relationship. They presented the cycle exhibited that Will would get upset and Stacy would withdraw for a day or two. The marriage was a first marriage for Will and a second marriage for Stacy. She'd grown up in a family with four older brothers who were physically abusive to her. Her father was a "drinker and a severe disciplinarian." He frightened Stacy. Her mother did not protect her from her brothers or her father. Stacy's first husband was alcoholic and also abused her. She left the marriage after four years. She had a three-year old daughter by that marriage. Will's father abandoned him and his mother when Will was four years old. Will was an only child and was especially close to his mother. She would refer to Will as "her little hero" as he grew up. Will was a self-admitted perfectionist. The cycle between them was that Will would get upset and "vent his frustration." Stacy would experience his emotional expression as anger and withdraw in fear. Will would pursue her, driving her further away. Will would then withdraw from Stacy, and the impasse could last for days. Will reported he knew that Stacy was afraid, but he didn't understand why she would be afraid of him. He loved her and would never hurt her.

After a number of sessions, I suggested that Will talk aloud with Stacy about his commitment to her, his desire to protect her, and his love for her. I reminded Will that he grew up in a home where he knew he was loved and cared for. Words and actions were communicated to him daily. Stacy had the opposite experience. Will said he knew her story, but figured she was with a very different man from her brothers, father, and first husband so she should know he loved her. I explained it didn't work like that. In fact, Stacy probably struggled with the idea of even deserving love, care, safety, and security. Will did start to express his commitment, protection, and love to Stacy verbally, daily. After two months of Will reaffirming his intentions, both reported the relationship was improving and the frequency of the fear/distance cycle had almost vanished. That's when Will asked me: "How long do I have to keep doing this (reaffirming messages) for her?" Stacy was hurt by the question—as if her interest and need for love and closeness with him was a problem or a burden. But instead of reacting defensively, Stacy jumped in and reminded Will that since he had started expressing more overtly his commitment, protection, and love to her, their relationship had improved markedly, they were talking more, the tension and distance had all but gone away, and they were making love more often, with Stacy initiating sex again. They were going out as a couple again. So, I asked:

Galvin: Will, am I understanding all of the progress in the relationship that Stacy just mentioned?

Will: Yes.

Galvin: Do you love Stacy and feel the things you say to her?

Will: Yes, of course.

Galvin: So, you mean the wonderful things you're saying, and both of you are making a positive difference in your marriage, and yet, somehow you feel like what you're doing is some kind of chore—like "it's work." Is that right?

Will: I just feel like her being so needy makes me worry about getting trapped into having to constantly reassure her. Shouldn't she be becoming more and more convinced that I love her. I shouldn't have to tell her all the time.

*"Time out." There are two explanations that come to my mind in understanding why men (and sometimes women) worry about building these reassuring messages (verbal and/or actions) into

their marriages: 1. Will mentioned fearing that he is "feeding" her neediness and her expectations will only grow. He experiences this as controlling and a "trap" he may not be able to keep up with; and the second reason I think of is: 2. The couple's reassurance "back and forth" exhausts Will as he tries to feel his own feelings as well as needing to feed her needs in the marriage. It opens up a feeling of vulnerability in him. This can be intolerable for some men (and women). But this is also why men sometimes turn feelings of anxiety into retreat, hurt into anger, and feelings of longing into lust.

Stacy jumped in and said she could understand his concerns, but reassured him that she is not feeling or needing more and more. What he is doing is wonderful and enough to make a big difference for her. She also knew this was hard for him because she could feel his vulnerability and understood that might frighten him. But she has never felt so "in this together" as she did now, and hoped they could keep working together. So, getting back to Will's question: "How long......?"

Galvin: Will, I want to answer your question. And after listening to the snippet of conversation you and Stacy just had I can say without hesitation: you get to do this with Stacy for the rest of your life.

They both laughed and Will recommitted himself to verbally love Stacy for the rest of their lives. And I repeat myself by saying: "Never forget Your wife wants to have a relationship with you."

REMEMBER:

You, as a husband, want to make a difference in your wife's life. And there is nothing she wants more than to hear, and see, and feel your words and actions that clearly state how important she is to you, and how much you love her. If you have gotten into the habit of neglecting or withholding your words and actions, you need to start, in your heart, to generate the feelings you have for her, wanting her to feel safe with you, and how much you love her. Start again to bring yourself to her and give her a chance to hear, and feel, and absorb your heartfelt love. She wants to give you a good response.

FOR WIVES ONLY:

What I'm suggesting to your husband may be difficult for him to do. Declare his heartfelt love for you. To open himself up and be vulnerable with you, fearing a "lukewarm" response, or worse yet, a rejection from you. Please remember that making changes can take time and we need to do things differently for a while before they settle in. It can be very scary for both of you. He's afraid he'll never be enough. And you, fearing he will start pursuing you for a relationship, and over time "change back" to being distant and avoidant. That's why I told Will the answer to his question is: "You get to pursue Stacy 'forever.'" I'm hoping now your husband is realizing he is in a relationship with you, and needs to commit himself to be an active, engaged, responsive, loving contributor to your marriage on a daily basis keeping it alive and vibrant but real. Please remember, your good response makes a big difference because you do!

Chapter Nine

"How do I get my wife to say "YES" to sex more often?"

THIS IS A question that men often ask themselves. Of course, there is no simple answer to that question, but let me share with you my experience with helping couples talk about coming to an understanding about their love life. There are certainly things men can do to interest their wives in making love more often, but first let me talk about three things men do (regularly), that makes their wife less interested.

The first thing we do to "turn her off" is use impersonal language.

*"Do you want to have sex tonight?"

*"How about having sex tonight?"

*"We haven't had sex in a long time—how about tonight?"

*"You never seem to be interested in having sex—can we have sex tonight?"

Sex, sex, sex, sex, sex, sex! Can you hear it? What do you imagine she hears when you use the "S" word constantly? Maybe a little objectified? Maybe that you are really only interested in an orgasm? And the "presentation," it feels like a "full court press" in basketball. Relentless at times.

I worked with a couple facing this issue. Owen was worried that Dana had lost all interest in him sexually. He worried that she felt no desire to be with him. I asked Dana if that was true, if she no longer felt desirous of him? She said "no," there were times when she thinks about him and feels very desirous. Owen was surprised to hear the news. He asked her why she never mentions it to him. She told him that he was so relentless in his pressing her for sex that it really turned her off to him, and she could not feel her desirous feelings when he pressured her that way. Dana said she usually felt her interest in him when she was alone and thinking about him and how much she loves him. She reported that this was usually when she was at work, alone in her office, during a quiet time of the day. I asked her if she would ever consider calling/texting/emailing Owen in those moments when she feels romantic, and share the feeling she is having in that moment with him? She said "No, I would never do that, are you kidding me?" I asked her why. Dana said, "If I called him and told him that, he would leave his office immediately and come find me to have sex, and that is not going to happen in my office!" They both laughed. Owen said, "She's right, I probably would do that."

This leads to the second thing men do to short circuit their sexual, love life with their wives; that is being totally unaware of how he's coming across to her in his approach. Husbands need to remember that sex is not an "event." And there is no "transactional" component to a couple's love life. Remember, to your wife the world is a relational place. That is how she sees and experiences the world she lives in, and that happens to be the world you live in, too. If you want to influence and engage your wife in any aspect of your marriage, you need to think relationally. So, you ask yourself, "What is she hearing when I approach her in a pressing, negative emotionally intense way?" Am I interested in her? Am I interested in our relationship? Am I interested in just having sex? Am I interested in having an orgasm? Try to imagine what it must be like for her on the other side.

And listen, I get it. A urologist at Washington University in St. Louis once was talking about women's and men's hormones. He noted that "we talk a lot about women's hormones because they are cyclical and are experienced and managed on a short cycle, but we don't talk about the fact that men deal with a constant, intense flow of testosterone surging through their bodies on a continuous basis." Research has shown that for men, three or four days after they make love with their wives, they begin to feel the desire to be sexual again. And the conflicted "dance" begins again.

That leads us to the third, and probably most impactful thing men do (or in this case, don't do) to negatively impact their love life with their wives. They do not tell their wives the real reason they are so adamant, pressing, insistent, difficult, and unreasonable in their approach to making love. One of the services I have provided in my work has been psycho-educational groups to men about marriage. One of the topics is "Men, Marriage, and Intimacy." During the lecture when we're talking about the couple's sex life, I ask the men to tell me what happens to them emotionally when they make love to their wife. "What feelings come up for you?" It does not take long to get a list. Here are sixteen of the most common words that describe their experience:

1. Loved; 2. Desired; 3. Close; 4. Warm; 5. Accepted; 6. Secure; 7. Seen; 8. Cared for; 9. Satisfied; 10. Caring; 11. Giving; 12. Happy; 13. Attractive; 14. Contented; 15. Appreciated; 16. Sexy.

The truth is that men feel their emotions for their wife most strongly and clearly when they're making love. But how many men have been aware of this and have talked to their wife about this extremely important experience? So, after I make the list, I asked the men in the room if the list represented their experience. Most all said "yes," or nodded their head. I then asked: "How many of you have spoken to your wife about this so she knows why it is so important to you?" Not one hand goes up. So, my next question was: "What do you think would happen if you went home and told her how you felt about her when she made love with you?" Crickets....... I knew one man in one of the groups I led. He must have gone home and told his wife what he felt when they made love, because about two weeks later I ran into her at the grocery store. Here is what she said to me: "I don't know exactly what you talked about at that meeting two weeks ago, but Jack came home and told me some loving things that have made life at our house really wonderful since then." It's obvious he went home and told her what it's like for him to be with her making love.

I'm sorry to have taken so long to get to this point in our conversation, but I wanted you to know that there are things we do, as husbands, that actually make things worse for ourselves and our wives in the area of intimacy. We need to stop the "full court press." We need to imagine what it must be like for her when we pressure her. How it sends an outrageously "unrelational" message to her that is hurtful, guilt inducing, shaming, and ultimately leads to frustration and anger for her, eroding her sense of safety and love with us. And finally, we have to tell our wives what it is really like for us to be close and loving with her. We, men, try to get our needs met without being vulnerable. That is a poor strategy if we hope to be in an intimate relationship. Intimacy requires vulnerability. We husbands need to let our wife know what a huge difference she makes in our lives, especially emotionally, and how much we need her. When a woman understands the positive, loving difference she makes, it opens her heart, and motivates her to want to give more in the relationship. But making love is only one of three ways that couples build intimacy.

The three intimacies are: 1. Verbal/emotional intimacy; 2. Physical/non-sexual intimacy; and 3. Sexual intimacy.

The verbal/emotional intimacy we covered in chapters two and three. Our presence, our interest, our attention, our listening, our understanding, our turning toward our wife, our making eye contact, our focusing on the relationship when we're talking with her, and our finding joy in her desire to tell us about her life in her stories. I think we covered that pretty well, so let's move on to physical/non-sexual affection.

Human touch is powerful. When our spouse touches us, we feel things that words could never evoke. A deep feeling that warms and soothes us. Holding hands; arms around each other; a good hug (at least 20 seconds); a six-second kiss (John Gottman says: "Now, that's a kiss."); a massage of your shoulders or feet; and lying close next to each other in bed, or spooning all create an emotional and bonding moment that builds a sense of connectedness couples look forward to. But, in my experience, men often act in a way that sabotages this intimacy by sexualizing it. In my practice, men are the ones who most complain about the lack of physical/non-sexual touch. The reason men complain about the lack of physical access to their wives is the same reason women have withdrawn from it. Men complain because she limits his "access" to her body. And the reason she does this is because he will try to use physical affection as foreplay. Wives usually feel his doing this diminishes her and makes the experience of touching uncomfortable for her. Once again, she finds herself in the position of resisting and saying "NO." Pushing him away and moving away from him to protect her integrity as a person and not an object. The cycle continues and once again he is pursuing hard and she is distancing. The problem is usually not with the woman (most women treasure physical affection), but instead, it is with the husband "sexualizing" affectionate touch.

Greg and Keesha had reached an impasse in their relationship. Greg had become sullen and withdrawn. They were not talking, and most of the conflict revolved around times when they were sexual, which was seldom and guarded.

Greg (to therapist): Something is wrong with her. She used to be so free and easy and loving and affectionate. Now she's become cold, and withholding, and almost punishing toward me when we have sex. She won't even let me touch her anymore. I call her the "ice queen."

***Time out, let me just say two things here. One is that calling your spouse a name never works out well. It just adds to the list of things you are going to have to apologize for later. And some names create damage that your spouse may never really be able to forget. The second thing is never using your spouse's parents' name (or titles) when you are in an argument. Like this: "You are just like your mother (Judy), or father (Stan)." In the dozens and dozens of times I've witnessed this, it has never turned out well. And it can also damage the in-law relationship if your wife feels you have contempt for her parents. So, try hard to avoid both. Ok, back to Greg and Keesha.

Keesha (to therapist): Did you hear that? Lovely. And this man wants to be closer to me. The "ice queen?" I don't think so. Let me tell you what this is really about. I have told him hundreds of times over the years and he has yet to listen to me, much less hear what I'm saying to him. As he said, I used to be open, and free and easy in our relationship. I love affectionate touch. Both giving and receiving it, but now whenever he touches me his hands go immediately to my breasts, or my butt, or between my legs. It's offensive to me that he wants to turn our loving touch into a session of him pawing me. I do not enjoy that and it reminds me that he just wants to be with me for one thing! And I resent that!!

I couldn't have said it better. Physical affection is not foreplay, and if we as husbands try to turn it into foreplay, it will disappear from our lives. Distance and disconnect will result and we will lose one of the three ways of intimacy in our marriages. And, if we sexualize affectionate touch, we are responsible for it, though we try to blame (and shame) our wives for it. We need to listen to her experience and understand how we are coming across to our wives. "What is the message she is getting from me, right now?"

As Keesha says: "He (Greg) turns our loving touch into a session of him pawing me….it reminds me that he just wants to be with me for one thing. I resent that!!" We, as husbands, may be smiling and playful when we "sexualize" affectionate touch, but that usually is not what she is feeling.

And now, the moment you have been waiting for, the third intimacy: the adult sexual relationship. I've heard men say that they think marriage 'kills" sex in a relationship. That is not true. One thing I've noticed in my practice is that in the dating and engagement period, men did more to pursue the woman in their lives for a relationship. When the marriage happened, they tended to pursue less. The pursuing makes a difference—daily. John Gottman found in his research that men tended to expect less in their marriage relationship. Actually, he said "men were content with less **(24)**." Except when it came to sex. So, husbands expect less in other areas of the relationship and don't pursue, but want more in the area of sex. It makes sense that the sexual relationship becomes the "battleground" in the marriage.

So, let me summarize: 1. We as husbands don't want to listen or talk much (be open-hearted and interested); 2. We "sexualize" affectionate touch; 3. We are content with less in the relationship (giving and receiving, except sex); 4. And we often "press hard" for sex. Ouch! Now, do you want to hear the good news?

As husbands, we can change all four of the things listed above because we are the major player in each one of them. In fact, we have more power than our wives do to change every one of them. Don't you think if our wives could "make us talk more, make us protect loving touch, make us be more driven to pursue and contribute to our relationship, and last but not least, make us tell her frequently what happens to us emotionally when we make love with her, and how deeply we need her, and love her in our lives, and what a difference she is"..........you get the point. She would do all of those things, if she could, and we would all be the happiest men on the planet! Right?? Now we know.

The sexual relationship allows the couple to love each other with their whole hearts and minds and bodies. The sexual relationship is the exclusive domain of the couple. No one else is involved. It is private and special and in a loving way, sacred. The couple builds a way to be together in a safe, comfortable, expressive, sensual, and satisfying way. It builds both physical and emotional closeness. It is personal, erotic, and exclusive. It is the "oasis" where the couple escapes all of the demands and expectations of life to be together and celebrate the loving relationship that strengthens their bond.

Don't forget, "Your wife wants to have a relationship with you."

REMEMBER:

I want to go back to the question at the very beginning: "How can I help my wife be more interested in having sex more often?" The answer to that question is all in our "perspective and attitude." Our perspective is now understanding that our sexual relationship is "embedded" (pun intended) in our intimate relationship. Our intimate relationship is composed of talking and sharing, touching in a loving and affectionate manner, and sharing our deep feelings and needs for our wife in our making love together. We also pursue her for time together, and take joy in listening to her opening up her life and thinking, and sharing that with us, so we can know and understand her better.

FOR WIVES ONLY:

This is tricky for me. Full disclosure, Kathy and I have had our fair share of conversations and "negotiations" about the frequency of our sexual relationship over the years. In most marriages it is not uncommon. My hope in writing this chapter is to provide a way for your husband to acknowledge and share with you his emotional experience when he makes love with you. I'm hoping in doing so you can understand better his "pressing" behavior in the past (it wasn't physical, it was his emotional needs driving him), so you and he can set a new relational course for a more open, loving future. You are very important to him. I'm hoping your husband works to be more aware of himself and your experience, so he can relate more open-heartedly and with less fear in your marriage.

TWO BONUS IDEAS AROUND PROTECTING YOUR INTIMACY:

The first idea is a common, daily problem I've heard from couples over my entire practice. Here is the question: *"My wife goes to bed early and I like to stay up later. We argue at times about her staying up with me, but when she does, she falls asleep on the couch and resents me for keeping her up. Sometimes she insists that I go to bed with her. I end up lying awake for hours after she has gone to sleep, and I end up resenting her. It's not a big problem, but it is a regular struggle for us. What should we do?"*

I appreciate the husband saying: "It's not a big problem, but a regular struggle for us." The more we, as couples, can manage our regular struggles, the least likely these problems are going to accumulate and result in the really big problem of: "We are not very compatible." It's not about compatibility as much, anyway. It's about our willingness and intention to work out our sharing life together and, as husbands, showing our wives our desire to give of ourselves in order to work things out.

So, here is the plan: You both go to bed together when the "early bird" goes to bed. The goal is to (1) eliminate the daily impasse (and the resentful feelings that go with it); (2) to start a quiet, connecting time for you and your wife to enjoy and share together every evening; and (3) for both parties to show their respect and support for each other, and their differences. Maybe the "night owl" gets ready for bed when the couple goes to bed, too, but only if their getting ready for bed later wakes your spouse up. The couple has the understanding that when the "early bird" goes to sleep (which they always do in short order), the "night owl" can get up and do whatever "night owls" do before they are ready to go to bed. The two reasons I think this is a good idea are: 1. You two can stop making this a daily point of conflict; and 2. You two can make this a "sweet time" for the two of you at the end of the day. Lying in bed together in the evening gives you a chance to talk, catch up, cuddle, and be close (every night). It's quiet, dark, and no one is busy doing anything else. Undistracted. Each of you is showing accommodation to the other, eliminating resentment. For husbands, doing this reflects your desire to be together and share in the relationship. Don't forget, your wife wants to be in a relationship with you.

The second idea, too, can involve moments in bed at night together. Let me just state the question presented by one client: *"One of the more uncomfortable moments, for me, in our marriage is when my wife and I are lying in bed and I ask (or "cue") my wife to have sex tonight, and she says "NO." She usually has some reason, but I feel rejected. It is a painful moment for me. I usually turn over and disengage from her. I feel rejected. How can I deal with those moments differently?"*

This is a scenario that occurs millions of times around the world every night. As the questioner said, he usually turns over. Frustrated. And your wife, lying next to you, can feel the tension and has to deal with the dilemma of trying to engage you, fearing the only thing that would make you happy is if she has sex with you. Yet, she's not feeling interested tonight (and worried if she did have sex, this could become a pattern in which she would feel "controlled" by your mood). At this moment, you are feeling hurt and rejected, but she thinks you're angry. A real dilemma for both of you. In my experience, this is usually the first time in the day your wife is aware that you were interested in having sex tonight—late in the day. (And let me be clear, she is well aware that you would like to have sex every night—but that's not going to happen). There is an old adage: "Foreplay begins at breakfast." What that means is in the morning when the day is starting the husband is "seeing, hearing, and appreciating" his wife and starting the relationship engagement from the start of the day.

*"Honey, what's your day look like?"

*"You look beautiful in that outfit; I think it's my favorite."

*"I can't wait to get home and catch up with you. We can talk."

*"Let's both call in sick today and run away together. Maybe no one will come and get us and make us come back. What do you think?"

Relational engagement. It begins with verbal/emotional intimacy. I see you. We are talking. I am interested in your day and your life. You! We are connected. I care about you. That's when it begins. We "stay" with her throughout the day. Calls, texts, emails, letting her know you can't wait to see her after work. As a husband, you need to create a "presence" with her and an anticipation of being back together. Women live in relationship. I've heard many women say to their husbands: "I know when you leave the house in the morning, I vanish! You don't think about me during your day. I'm 'out of sight, out of mind.'" Not good. We love our wives and need to be more intentional and purposeful in communicating that clearly, on a daily basis.

Now, let's go back to the bedroom scene. We need to know that this moment in bed now is one of those "important moments" in our marriage when we need to be paying attention, and do something different. She says "NO." Instead of being mad, we need to be curious. She says "NO," and we stay with her. Do not turn over. Trying to soothe your hurt feelings and feeling rejected, but we say:

Husband: Do you want to make love tonight?

Wife: No, I'm really tired tonight.

Husband (soothing himself and staying with her): Did anything in particular happen today that took so much out of you?

Wife: Yes, we had a meeting late in the afternoon that was quite stressful. I don't think I ever recovered.

Husband: Are you ok? Has it kind of stayed with you?

Wife: Yeah. I've been thinking about it off and on all evening. I don't know what I'm going to do about it.

Husband: That's not like you. This must have been something very difficult. I'm sorry that happened to you. Is there anything I can do for you?

Wife: Thank you, that's sweet of you. Let me see what happens tomorrow, maybe we can talk about it after dinner tomorrow night, if it's still so intense and bothering me.

Husband: Sure, we can. Come over here and let me hug you. Then you can get some sleep. I love you.

After that exchange, she feels it. She feels his love and care for her. A very different outcome from his turning over hurt and "mad." Guys, that's what you are trying to create in these moments. A very different outcome—for both of you! You have to manage and contain your desire and expectation for sex at that moment. She knows, and you know, making love is on your mind. What is the message you want to give her in this critical moment? Gentlemen, you can do this. Your message to your wife at that moment is: 1. "You are not alone;" 2. "I'm right here. Now;" 3. "I am paying attention;" 4. "I want to know how you are doing (curious);" and 5. "I care about you." You communicate these things through your actions, words, and attitude. Don't forget your wife wants to have a relationship with you.

Chapter Ten

"Why is she always coming at me with a list of problems?"

Or put another way: "Why does my wife always bring up problems in our marriage and family? She always seems to find things to worry about." Mary and Tom came to see me. They had recently attended one of John Gottman's couple's weekend seminars and found it very helpful. However, Mary was disturbed by one statistic Gottman reported from his studies *(25)*, and that was "eighty-six percent of the time it is women who initiate problem-talk in a marriage." Mary agreed that in their marriage she brought problems up much more than did Tom. She wanted that to change.

Mary: Tom, it upsets me to hear Gottman's research because in our marriage I do bring up 86% of the problems—if not more. It isn't fair and I want you to bring up more problems. (Tom sat silent).

Galvin: Tom, did you hear what Mary just said?

Tom: Yes.

Mary: Tom, I want this to be more balanced. I want you to bring up more problems in our relationship so we can talk about what bothers you, too.

Galvin: Tom, do you understand what Mary is asking for? What thoughts come to you about her request?

Tom: No, I hear her, but I don't know what to do. (looking at Mary): What kinds of problems do you want me to bring up? A lot of the things you bring up as problems I'm not even aware of, much less thinking about. I'm pretty content with our relationship.

Mary: I know. That's what I'm talking about. I want you to start paying closer attention to what's going on between us—and the kids.

I have heard other wives ask their husbands to pay attention and bring up problems they are concerned about in their marriage. What is a problem? Who sees it? Who is concerned enough to bring it up first?

Let me tell you a few things I have come to understand about couples and why Gottman's 86% number is what it is.

As I have mentioned, women think about relationships ten times more than men do. Women's lives are oriented around relationships. Lavi and Rachel came to see me. They were in the waiting room before we started. When I went to bring them into my office, Lavi was mentioning to Rachel that he had run into an old friend (Ben) at lunch that afternoon. Rachel was very excited because Ben and his family used to be neighbors and she was close to Ben's wife, Helena.

Rachel: Oh my, honey that is great. We haven't seen them in months. How is Ben? How is Helena?

Lavi: Ben's doing great. He got a new job last summer and is working for that large accounting firm downtown. He seems very happy there.

Rachel: That's great! How's Helena?

Lavi: I don't know, I didn't ask.

Rachel: How about the kids? Their oldest started high school last fall? And their middle daughter was having some health problems when we moved.

Lavi: I don't know. They never came up. But Ben's firm has baseball tickets and said he might get them and take us to a game.

Rachel: That's nice. But Helena and the kids never came up? Did you ask about them?

Lavi: No, we were too busy catching up with our work and golf games. I never could beat him, remember?

Rachel: How long did you guys talk?

Lavi: Probably about a half hour or so. He has lost some weight and joined that gym in the old neighborhood.

Rachel: You talked a half hour and didn't find out about Helena or the family?

Sound familiar? Historically, women have been expected to be responsible for the relationships in the marriage and the family. That's an important responsibility, one that most women want to be involved in, but not by herself. So, when we look at the roles that men and women play in families, women tend toward: monitoring health and safety, watching developmental progress (or difficulties) of family members, and connection and love in the relationships. In short, safety, development, and connection (men, on the other hand, tend to focus more on providing, protecting, and loving family members). I'm going to focus on women's roles because it is important for men to know and understand what motivates women, and what their concerns are.

Let me be clear, I do not see these roles as exclusive to either gender. I have worked with many couples where the roles were reversed, and with many single parents who had to pay attention to everything going on in their families, sometimes alone. The fact is, every couple needs to pay attention to four tasks on a daily basis: 1. Running a household; 2. Making and managing money; 3. Taking care of children; 4. And having a loving relationship together. The wife and husband both need to participate in all four tasks in a cooperative way, daily. Women pay attention to how each family member looks and feels. They closely monitor health and safety concerns that arise. And it's a good thing because I have worked with numerous couples in which the woman's concerns and instincts have saved the lives of their husbands and/or one of their children, not to mention averting more serious medical complications. In marriages and families, the woman's awareness makes a big difference.

Secondly, women monitor family members for developmental milestones. How is everyone doing emotionally, physically, socially, academically, spiritually, psychologically, and relationally? Women are not just paying attention, they are "interventionalists." When they see a concern, they want to do something about it. I oversaw a clinic that saw families focusing on evaluating and treating developmental problems in children and adolescents. Eighty percent of the problems were around boys between the ages of five to eleven years old, presenting with ADHD. Ninety percent of the parents initiating the evaluation were moms.

And finally, women are paying attention to how much love, attention, support, and time family members are getting within the family. It is not unusual for wives to encourage their husbands to spend more time interacting and talking with their children. They do this because they know that for their kids to have time and attention with Dad is invaluable. That too, is why as a wife, she pursues a relationship with her husband. She feels time and attention to each other is essential to their relationship. She's right.

I don't want to get "too wordy" here, but I want you to understand how your wife sees the world and feels responsible (relationally) to "be a difference" in the lives of those she loves. That motivates her. She is not "looking for problems;" it's just that she "cannot not see" what she feels important for her to make sure is working well. That is a good thing for both your marriage and your family life.

So, let's talk about problem-talk in your marriage. So, your wife feels concerned about her relationship with you. When she feels concerned, she brings it to you because she: 1. Believes you will be interested; 2. Believes that you will want to talk and understand why it is a concern for her; 3. Believes you do not want her to feel alone worrying about the concern (that you will want to be there with her); and 4. Believes that you will want to brainstorm with her to figure out what to do about the concern going forward (you will want to be part of the solution with her). It is a tremendous act of confidence, faith, and hope that she is acting on her "belief" in all of those things about you. You need to give her a good response. As we heard Mary say earlier, paying attention, being concerned, and being the one who brings up problems (86% of the time) is a "burden" for her. This is an important role your wife plays. To minimize, negate, and dismiss her concern "piles on" another problem for her: she's alone, she's not taken seriously, and maybe she is "seen as the problem" by you. Can you imagine what that does to her trust in you?

This is a good time to remind husbands that ninety percent of everything that comes out of your wife's mouth is personal about her. She is sharing her perspective, her experience, her concerns, and her heart with you at that moment. Your job is not to judge or blame her, or defend yourself, or dismiss her, but to be curious and ask questions about what she sees, what she knows, what she is worried might happen, what the two of you might think about doing together, that's your job. To listen, understand, empathize, feel compassion (and caring) for her, and respond with kindness in the moment. If you do that, she will not feel alone, and you don't have to fear rejection because you are moving closer to her at a vulnerable moment in her life.

*"Yes, I see what you're saying?"

*"Can you tell me more about what you're worried about? And what you fear might happen?"

*"I'm not sure I fully understand your concern right now, but I'm so glad you are telling me about it because I never want you to feel alone with things that concern both of us, or to feel you can't talk to me."

Typically, your wife is not trying to control you; she is not trying to be "right" or trying to get her way; she's not intending to be negative, critical or blaming of you; or rejecting you. Giving her a "good response" is leading with your heart-felt good intention. You love your wife and want to be there with and for her. It is not easy to move toward your wife when she's upset. In fact, every "cell in your body" is telling you to move the other direction, but this is a very important moment to be there, and be available.

I worked with a couple, Tyler and Susan. Tyler had "perfected" the avoidant and dismissive response to Susan. They came in to see me because the distance that had developed between them was drifting toward a separation.

Susan: I love Tyler, but I can't reach him. It is as if we live two separate lives and just share space, really. It has gotten to where my loneliness in the marriage is much worse than what I imagine my loneliness would be in living alone. If I was lonely living alone, at least my loneliness would make more sense to me.

We worked together for a number of months, working on the patterns that maintained the distance and disconnect between them. Then one evening, Susan had had an especially brutal day at work. When she entered the house, she stood in the front foyer and started to cry (she later said it was the relief and release of being home). Tyler had gotten home an hour earlier and started dinner. He heard Susan come through the doorway and walked to the doorway of the dining room, looking toward the front door. He saw Susan crying, and since Susan hadn't seen him yet, Tyler's first thought was to slip downstairs, away from her. Tyler reports he heard MY voice in his head:

Galvin's voice: "Tyler, move toward her. She's hurting. She needs you. This is one of those really important moments we have talked about. Move toward her."

Tyler reported HIS voice in his head was saying: "Tyler, dude, you can still get downstairs. Susan hasn't seen you yet. Get to the basement. She will cry it out and you can talk later. She might be upset with YOU right now. She may be angry with YOU, dude."

Before he knew it, Tyler said he was moving across the living room toward the front door. He said it felt like "walking into machine gun fire" (a little dramatic, Tyler, but OK).

Susan saw Tyler and her crying intensified. She was sobbing.

Tyler's voice in his head was saying: "Galvin, you had better be right about this. If this ends badly, you are so fired!"

When Tyler reached Susan and put his arms around her, she fell into his arms. He held her as she cried, and he soothed her with loving comments. They both reported they had "the best evening" they had had in years. As Susan Johnson says: Be available, be responsive, and be engaged *(26)*. Don't forget: your wife wants to have a relationship with you.

REMEMBER:

Dan Wile says: "We solve the moment, not the problem *(27)*." Or maybe we solve the fear in the moment, and that solves the problem (being upset and being alone). What we know is that couples solve the problems in their lives best when there is an attentive, caring, supportive relationship and they can share in the process. We, as men, can be part of such a relationship if we will "learn to talk back to our own fears about our wives." We need to stop reacting to her with defensiveness, blaming, avoidance, and anger. Our wives need us. She comes to us for that reason and we need to move toward her with open arms, an open mind, and most of all an open heart. Her coming to us is a "vote of confidence," and a compliment. Don't miss it.

FOR WIVES ONLY:

I know how important your marriage is to you. I know how important it is for you to not feel alone in your marriage. I want you to understand that your husband does not experience "problem-talk" the way you do. Women are usually energized (I'm not saying happy) when they sit with their husbands and work together to deal with the extremely important issues, worries, and concerns in their relationship (or family life). Nothing is more important to you. But your husband will not be energized. He will be more distressed because he's tuned into your upset and worry. John Gottman found in his "love lab" when couples were dealing with emotionally charged issues, the husband would be flooded (heart rate over 100 bpm, perspiring, skin temperature rising), while the wife's physical state remained steady. This is why husbands try to "manage and contain" their wife's distressed feelings by saying things like:

*"It will be ok."

*"That's not a problem."

*"Don't worry about it, we will take care of it by doing _____."

He's hoping to regulate his distressed feeling by "trying to manage and contain" your distressed feelings. Like he could "talk you out of" what you're concerned about. It never works. I just want you to be aware of what he's trying to do and why he is doing it. When you're engaged in problem talk, he needs to work to regulate his own feelings. Breathing. Taking a short break. Talking to himself and reassuring himself ("No one has ever died from upset feelings."). But you can add your voice to his by saying things like:

*"I really appreciate you talking to me about this."

*"I love you and know you don't want me to worry alone."

*"It makes me feel safe and loved when we talk about our problems together. I know this isn't always easy for you, but it means everything to me. I love you."

Be your relational self.

THIRD AND FINAL TIME-OUT (THIRTY SECONDS)

Thirty seconds?!? I'd better get talking. Let's slow things down again and catch our breath. How are you holding up? I know we just covered a number of important topics in a short period of time. I hope you are not feeling overwhelmed by it all. It is important information to know, but don't put an expectation on yourself that you need to work all of this into your marriage today. I would again ask you to think about the topics or ideas that stood out for you. Which ones do you think are the most important ones to try to work on first? Start a conversation with your wife about your ideas and ask for hers. What do you need to begin to work on together? What outcome in your relationship would encourage you the most? Could you work with your wife on these areas together (besides more sex——she already knows that's always on the top of your list)? Tell her what it is that you're hoping to have happen between you by talking and working together. Ask the same question to her. Initiate a conversation. There—you two have already started planning and working things out together.

I just heard the whistle. Time out is over. Let's get back to the action.

Chapter Eleven

"You automatically make a difference in your marriage. You decide whether that difference will be the positive difference you want it to be."

HERE WE ARE at the end. I want to leave you with a number of bullet points to take with you as you pursue and engage your wife in your marriage:

1. Your marriage is a love relationship. Be loving with your wife in your attitude, intentions, and actions.

2. This is how the human brain works: what we focus on, we amplify. If we focus on the negative, that's what we amplify in our thinking and lives.

3. We are all "quirky." We need to give and receive grace, mercy, and love in our marriage relationship. As husbands we can lead in these areas.

4. Men: if the problem your wife is talking to you about involves you, that is great news. It's hard for you to positively

change or impact things in her life when you have no control over whatever might be bothering her; but if you are part of her concerns, there are a lot of things you can do to change the situation. Don't get defensive. Get Curious!

5. Paying attention and listening are more important than thinking. When you listen, you learn and can understand things with and about her. You open your heart and mind to her. Your wife needs you to be open-minded and open-hearted with her.

6. We all struggle at times with the universal question: "Am I loveable?" You can answer that question for your wife every single day. When you reminded her how much you love her, and how much she means to you, she will give you a good response. Encouragement and reassurance only strengthen a marriage.

7. Married couples need to develop a way of being together that they can maintain in a sustainable relationship together. A husband does that by "seeing, hearing, and appreciating" his wife every day.

8. Physical touch (non-sexual affection) communicates love and caring in a way words can never express. As a husband, we need to protect and foster affectionate touch.

9. John Gottman found in his studies that human beings need a 5 to 1 ratio of positive to negative responses in their marital interactions for the marriage to be more positive and secure *(29)*. In other words, for every one negative response to her there should be at least five positive responses.

10. Your wife shares more of the important relationships in your life with you than anyone else on the planet. Another good reason to nurture your partnership.

11. A "bad apology" evokes feelings of anger, guilt, and shame in your wife. Anger—because she's hurt and you seem not to care; Guilt— because your response says: "you are making a 'mountain out of a molehill' here; and shame— because your "bad apology" tells her that she doesn't deserve a serious response from you. Remember: Lo Seinto. "I feel you…."

12. We are working to build trust in our marriage. Anything we do to break trust needs to be repaired.

13. Men often see sex as the barometer for how the relationship is going. This point of view "dooms" us to focusing all of our efforts on having more, better sex so "things are better." It doesn't work. Sex (making love) is only a part of the "trilogy of intimacy." At the core of intimacy is Love, not sex. Talking, emotional engagement, and affection are the preambles to a loving sex life, not the other way around.

14. A marriage is a love relationship; a relationship of the heart.

15. Loving relationships contribute to longevity, better physical health, and better mental health for both partners *(30)*. Be active and intentional about your love, and your need to be loved.

16. Six things that "get in the way" of good marriages:

   a. "Busy and tired." We are all busy and tired. Somehow we find a way to manage those two problems away from the loving and parenting of our kids, but we are less likely to manage them away from our couple time together. We need to be more intentional in that area with our spouse.

   b. "Taking each other for granted." When we neglect our relationship, negativity begins to creep in. The sad thing is we love each other and do things each day to "take care of our marriage," but we don't do them in a personal way that focuses our attention and love to our spouse.

   c. Too much "screen time, work time, other activities, and/or other relationships" can dilute the attention and engagement desired by both parties to support and sustain their love relationship. All of these things can be important and "good things to do," but they need to be talked about and managed together so they don't come across as "more important" than our marriage, or our relationship with our wife.

   d. Don't stop "dating." When I say this I mean finding time to be together and talk, or share an activity, alone where the focus is just on the two of you, and the relationship both of you need.

   e. Try to have other couples in your lives. Being a couple as part of a larger couple's group of friends is an important way to experience your relationship together, through the eyes of other couples who care about you.

   f. Do not let the "consumer culture" mentality (31)

of the world change in any way your perspective of your marriage. The "consumer culture" thinking says to your wife "what have you done for me lately?" It doesn't have you loving your wife, but instead, it has you "consuming" her. Our attitude and perspective are: "My job is to be the best husband I can be, which means I'm present to her, listening, being understanding and empathic, acting with compassion and kindness." That is my perspective and attitude. Tell yourself these things daily. You are important to your wife. She loves you and needs to know you want to be with her, and be in a relationship with her. Never forget your wife wants to be in a relationship with you. That is great news!

17. Remember, at the heart of every good marriage there are three attitudes we need to keep in mind: 1. GRACE—that is giving our wife more "good intentions" (the benefit of the doubt) in our interactions with her than we think she might deserve, in the moment. 2. MERCY—that is interacting with our wife always remembering that she is vulnerable with us because we are so important to her. And 3. LOVE—that is always keeping in mind the bond that connects us, and we are working to never doing, or saying, anything that would compromise that bond. We are with her because we love her.

REMEMBER:

Ok, I've been blathering on for eleven chapters already. I want to get down to the real reason why this is important to you, your wife, your family, and your life. You two are on the most important adventure of your lifetime. Life is long, and there are many things that are going to happen to you (good and difficult); individually and as a couple (parents, too). In those moments you are going to need someone to hang onto in order to get through the challenges, and to hang onto and celebrate the great moments. Life is long, and we don't know what is ahead for us. But one thing we can provide for each other is "good company" for the journey. No one has to endure this alone! As I have mentioned, no one takes care of a marriage but the two people in it. Oh, everyone counts on you as a couple, but they "pull you in directions for their needs, not yours." I've always told couples: "Your young children will suck the marrow out of your bones if you let them; and your older kids will suck all of the money out of your bank account, if you let them." Ha!

Truth is, most of the marriage relationship is spent on the "back side of raising children." That's when the couple is alone together (again) and has time and resources (hopefully) to spend a good deal of time together and celebrate the successful first half of their marriage. That's right! At this point, a couple can have 25 to 30 good years of being together, loving each other, and enjoying themselves together. We need each other for both parts. That's what we pledged to do. "For better or worse; for richer or poorer; in sickness and health; as long as we both shall live!" And that's a promise we need to keep and nourish every day. "The ball is in your court," gentlemen. You can do this. Go and love your wife! And don't ever forget: Your wife wants to have a relationship with YOU!

FOR WIVES ONLY:

I have tried to capture the essence of what I've come to understand a marriage relationship, from my experience, looks like. Over the years, I have tried to bring home things I have learned and to talk with Kathy about them, so we could figure out together how we could use these ideas to strengthen our marriage. I encourage you now to take from this book the ideas and actions that stand out to you, what's important to you, and how these things make sense to you; so, you and your husband can talk about and build in what you need together to make your marriage stronger, more secure, and more loving. Thank you for paying close attention to finding what in this book is important to you and talking to your husband about that. Marriage is the foundation of civilization. Thank you for "staying with me" throughout the book. I hope it has made a difference in your thinking about yourself, your husband, and your marriage, too.

Appendix A:

I would say "this is your homework," but it is so much more than that. I have mentioned a number of times your need, as a husband, to "see, hear, and appreciate" your wife. The way you do this is by telling her (out loud and/or in writing) the things you notice and love about her. I have listed many qualities below that I suggest you go through to identify those that relate to your wife. I have also listed a number of stem sentences to give you ideas about how you would say these many things you see in her, and know about her, that you love and appreciate about her. I would suggest you find ways to communicate these to her on a daily basis (verbally, and/or with notes, emails, texts, soap writing messages on the bathroom mirror……maybe not that one). The point is: you are now paying attention and intentionally contributing, in a positive way, to your relationship with her daily. And this communication is coming straight from your heart! Actually, this isn't homework, per se, it is: ***the rest of my life's work of love!*** Make it daily, and make it fun for both of you!

*What I love about being married to you is: _____
_____
_____.

*The characteristics you bring to our relationship that I love the most are:_____
_____.

*Have I told you lately how much _____ inspires me.

*I need to feel, and I do feel, _____ every day. Thank you for bringing that to our marriage.

*I appreciate _____. I'm so glad I'm married to you!

1. You're loving me; 2. Your wisdom; 3. Your courage; 4. Your sense of style; 5. Your thoughtfulness; 6. Your affection; 7. Your loyalty to us; 8. Your generosity to others; 9. The way you kiss me; 10. Your energy; 11. Your sense of humor; 12. Your decisiveness in key situations; 13. Your creative imagination; 14. How interested you are to know me; 15. Your smile; 16. How safe I feel with you; 17. Your consideration of me; 18. Your support for things I do in my life; 19. Your enthusiasm; 20. Your consideration for me and others; 21. Your thoughtfulness in managing our resources; 22. The way you accept me for who I am; 23. Your gratitude and appreciation for where we are in our lives together; 24. Your playfulness, 25. Your cheerfulness; 26. Your caring; 27. Your reliability; 28. Your openness with me; 29. Your taking responsibility in your life and in our marriage; 30. Your gentleness; 31. Your Kindness. 32. Your faith; 33. Your ways of being romantic in our

marriage; 34. And you can add any (and all) qualities you "hear, see, feel, and love" about your wife here:_____ _____.

Appendix B:

I want to talk about marriage therapy for a moment. It is usually the wife in the marriage who brings up the suggestion that she thinks the two of you might benefit from seeing a marriage therapist. Ninety percent of the intake calls to me for marriage therapy are made by women. This is a very important time for you as a husband to pay close attention. It was not uncommon when I started working with a couple that the wife would mention that she started suggesting marriage counseling one, two, or three years prior. The reason she is suggesting going together is because she's beginning to feel that the two of you cannot talk together, understand each other, and resolve the impasse she sees to your being closer in your relationship. As I've mentioned before, women are monitoring the relationships (and how things are going) in the home. This is with both the children and the marital relationship. When your wife sees something that "looks like trouble," or concerns her, she wants to do something about it right away, and not let it get worse. For the husband, the idea of marriage therapy is the "nightmare" that you will be sitting in an office with two women talking about your wife's hurt feelings and your bad behavior. It's usually for this reason that when the wife calls me she will say she is calling me because her husband would come only if they saw a male therapist. I'm here to tell you that I have known and worked with dozens of excellent women marital therapists who worked to make each person in the couple feel understood and safe. I think it's important for you to know that the last thing your wife wants by going together to marriage therapy is for things to get worse between you. I am very certain about that. So, it would be helpful, before you go to your first session, to talk about what each of you hopes to see happen as a result of your time talking together with the therapist. Ask her what she hopes you can work on and accomplish together. Then tell her what you hope you can accomplish as a couple in the work you will do together. Just an aside: Do not say "you just want her to be happy." We all want our spouses to be happy, but saying that might come across as your' suggesting: 1. That her not being happy is the problem—if she would just get happy, all would be well; and 2. You are satisfied with how things are and you can't think of anything that includes both of you doing something different together to strengthen your relationship connection. Tell her something that you want to do to make things better between you, and ask her if that would make a difference to her. You matter to her. She needs to know you think about your marriage and how to work to improve things, too.

Let me say a few things about the process of marital therapy. Therapy is a conversation. It is a conversation with a purpose. You and your wife are going together, sharing the same goal—a closer, more effective partnership. Make sure she knows you are on board with that goal. Therapy is an exploration of patterns and dynamics in your relationship that both interfere with you being closer, as well as ways to build (and keep) closeness in your relationship. It's not unlike what you have just read in the first three chapters (building closeness) and the second three chapters (things that interfere with a close relationship). I said therapy is a conversation with a purpose. In that way it is not unlike the process we talked about in chapter two: listening to her, working to understand her better, feeling what it must be like to be in her "shoes," feeling compassion for her, and responding with kindness and love—and vice versa. If the two of you find yourself with a therapist who is not bringing these elements to the work, then find another therapist. I have referenced a number of marital therapy approaches that have a good success history in helping couples restore the love and connection in their lives. Marital therapy should feel "safe" for all involved. The approaches are: 1. The Gottman Method; 2. Emotionally-Focused Couple's Therapy; 3. Imago Therapy; and 4. Internal Family Systems Therapy (IFS). You can ask the therapist if they practice with any of these. The best way to find a good marital therapist is to ask friends if they know of, or have seen, a couple's therapist (usually your wife will do better asking her friends than you might in asking your friends). Once you find a couple's therapist, remember, you are not going alone. You are going with your wife. She wants the experience to be positive and contribute to making your relationship stronger and more intimate. You are going together with the same goal. Everyone is a little nervous at first (including the therapist, who never knows what's going to happen), but as I mentioned, it's the therapist's job to create a sense of safety and comfort for all involved so that work can be achieved. After each session, you and your wife can talk about what you think happened and what was the most helpful part for you both. Remember, you are in this together. It is your marriage and your life you are working to improve. Nothing is more important at that time, and your wife wants to have a relationship WITH YOU!

Suggested Readings

(Books you might want to read together).

John Gottman, Ph.D.

1. The Seven Principles for Making Marriage Work. John M. Gottman, Ph.D.

2. What Makes Love Last? John M. Gottman, Ph.D.

Susan Johnson, Ed.D.

1. Hold Me Tight: Seven Conversations for a Lifetime of Love. Dr. Susan Johnson

2. Love Sense: The Revolutionary New Science of Romantic Relationships. Dr. Susan Johnson

Daniel B. Wile, Ph.D.

1. After the Fight: Using Your Disagreements to Build a Stronger Relationship. Daniel B. Wile, Ph.D.

Hartville Hendrix, Ph.D.

1. Getting the Love You Want: A Guide for Couples. Harville Hendrix, Ph.D. and Helen LaKelly Hunt, Ph.D.

2. Making Marriage Simple: Ten Relationship-Saving Truths. Harville Hendrix, Ph.D. and Helen LaKelly Hunt, Ph.D.

Janis Abrams Spring, Ph.D.

1. After the Affair: Third Addition. Janis Abrams Spring, Ph.D.

Daniel Siegel, M.D.

1. Mindsight, Daniel Seigel, M.D.

William Doherty, Ph.D.

1. Take Back Your Marriage, William Doherty, Ph.D.

References

1. John Gottman, PhD., et.al, THE MAN'S GUIDE TO WOMEN, Rodel Wellness @ 2016, page 5.

2. John Gottman, PhD., et al., THE MAN'S GUIDE TO WOMEN, Rodel Wellness @ 2016, Pgs. 138-139

3. Harville Hendrix, PhD., GETTING THE LOVE YOU WANT, Owl Books @2001, Pgs. 142-153.

4. John Gottman, PhD., THE SEVEN PRINCIPLES FOR MAKING MARRIAGE WORK, Crown Books @1999, Pg. 130

5. Harville Hendrix, PhD., THROUGH CONFLICT TO CONNECTION, Imago Video Training Series, @IRI 2006.

6. Susan Johnson, EdD., EMOTIONALLY FOCUSED THERAPY, Pesi Video Series, October 27, 2014.

7. Susan Johnson, EdD., EMOTIONALLY FOCUSED

THERAPY, Pesi Video Series, October 27, 2014.

8. Deborah Tannen, PhD., YOU JUST DON'T UNDERSTAND, William Morrow and Co., Inc., @1990, Pg. 76

9. Conversation with Olga Silverstein, MSW (The Ackerman Institute, NYC) at the Family Therapy Summer Institute in St. Louis, MO, 1988.

10. John Gottman, PhD., THE SEVEN PRINCIPLES FOR MAKING MARRIAGE WORK, Crown Books @ 1999, Pg. 26.

11. John Gottman, PhD., THE SEVEN PRINCIPLES FOR MAKING MARRIAGE WORK, Crown Books @ 1999, Pgs. 109-110.

12. Michael Yapko, PhD., BREAKING THE PATTERNS OF DEPRESSION, APA Video Training Series, @2005

13. Michael Yapko, PhD., BREAKING THE PATTERNS OF DEPRESSION, APA Video Training Series, @ 2005.

14. John Gottman, PhD. Lecture given at Mercy Medical Center, St. Louis, MO, 1998.

15. John Gottman, PhD., THE SEVEN PRINCIPLES FOR MAKING MARRIAGE WORK, Crown Books @ 1999, Pgs. 29-34.

16. Susan Johnson, EdD., EMOTIONALLY FOCUSED THERAPY, Pesi Video Series, October 27, 2014.

17. Betty Carter, MSW, WHO'S IN THE KITCHEN, Steven Lehrner Productions @

18. Rick Hanson, PhD., HARDWIRING HAPPINESS, Pesi Video Series. October 15, 2014.

19. Harville Hendrix, PhD., THROUGH CONFLICT TO CONNECTION, Imago Video Training Series, IRI Production @2006.

20. Tod Bolsinger, CANOEING THE MOUNTAINS, IVP Standard Edition @2015.

21. Janice Spring, PhD., AFTER THE AFFAIR, Harper Collins @ 2020.

22. Kathleen McVoy, MSW, MENNINGER FOUNDATION MARRIAGE AND FAMILY THERAPY TRAINING LECTURE SERIES, St. Louis, MO, 1990.

23. John Gottman, PhD., WHAT MAKES LOVE LAST?, Simon and Schuster @2012, Pgs. 67-80.

24. John Gottman, PhD., Lecture given at Mercy Medical Center, St. Louis, MO, 1998.

25. John Gottman, PhD., MAKING RELATIONSHIPS WORK, DVD, The Gottman Institute @ 2010.

26. Susan Johnson, EdD., HOLD ME TIGHT, Little, Brown, and Co. @ 2008.

27. Dan Wile, PhD., SOLVING THE MOMENT, Dorothy

Kaufmann @ 2021.

28. John Gottman, PhD., MAKING RELATIONSHIPS WORK, DVD, The Gottman Institute @ 2010.

29. John Gottman, PhD., MAKING RELATIONSHIPS WORK, DVD, The Gottman Institute @ 2010.

30. Daniel Seigel, MD., ATTACHMENT, TRAUMA, AND PSYCHOTHERAPY, Pesi Video Series, March 24, 2020.

31. William Doherty, PhD., TAKE BACK YOUR MARRIAGE, The Guilford Press @ 2001.

Acknowledgements

Personally, I want to thank my wife, Kathy, for her love and devotion to working in our marriage with me for forty-seven years. None of this would have been possible without her. I want to thank my three sons Ben, Michael, and Jonathan for helping me learn that the more love I have given them, the more love they have given back to me. I'm thankful for our daughter-in- law, Sarah and our grandson, Shiloh, and our soon-to-be daughter-in-law, Angela for helping me understand and know how love and relationships stretch and grow as families grow. I love you all and appreciate your love and support. Thank you!

On the professional front, I want to thank all of the colleagues I have practiced with over the years: Kathy McVoy, Leslie Gennari, Joyce Coleman, Liz Schwarz, Gail Gordon, Greg Krueger, Bob Lewis, and Jerry Tullman. You have supported me and my work, as well as given great companionship and encouragement. Thank You!

I want to thank the fifty colleagues who have participated in our READING AND VIDEOTAPE DISCUSSION SEMINARS, meeting monthly for the last twenty-three years. We have read and discussed books, watched endless videos, talked about our work, talked about our lives, and grown up together. I told all of you that I learned so much more from you than you did from me. The St. Louis MFT Community has been a rich, caring, and supportive group of committed professionals that have made me a better therapist and person throughout the years. Thank you!

I want to thank Mary Wertsch for helping me find "my voice," and introducing me to "the guy" sitting next to me, who I spoke to as I wrote; and to Taylor McKenna for his expertise and timely assistance with everything technical; and to Tom and Julia Bakewell for their availability, feedback, and research they provided, that encouraged me along the way. Thank you!

Also, I would like to thank Marta Papa, J.D. who always supported my writing, and Bill Bumberry, Ph.D. who hosted a decade of seminars with the leading MFT thinkers in the field. Thank you!

Finally, I want to thank John Gottman for teaching me how marriages work. I want to thank Olga Silverstein for teaching me the value and complexity of relationships. And I want to thank Susan Johnson for teaching and helping me better understand connection and love! They all provided the "building blocks" that helped me write this book. Thank you!

Printed in the USA
CPSIA information can be obtained
at www.ICGtesting.com
LVHW051149210324
774706LV00004B/11